D0402184

BLACK-BROWN RELATIONS AND STEREOTYPES

BLACK-BROWN

RELATIONS AND STEREOTYPES

Tatcho Mindiola Jr.,
Yolanda Flores Niemann,
and Nestor Rodriguez

University of Texas Press, Austin

Copyright © 2002 by the University of Texas Press
All rights reserved
Printed in the United States of America

First edition, 2002

Requests for permission to reproduce material from this
work should be sent to Permissions, University of Texas Press,
Box 7819, Austin, TX 78713-7819.

♾ The paper used in this book meets the minimum
requirements of ANSI/NISO Z39.48-1992
(R1997) (Permanence of Paper).

Library of Congress Cataloging-in-Publication Data

Mindiola, Tatcho.
Black-brown relations and stereotypes / Tatcho Mindiola Jr.,
Yolanda Flores Niemann, and Nestor Rodriguez.
p.   cm.
Includes bibliographical references and index.
ISBN 0-292-75264-4 (cloth : alk. paper) — ISBN 0-292-75268-7
(pbk. : alk. paper)
1. African Americans—Texas—Houston—Relations with Hispanic
Americans.   2. Hispanic Americans—Texas—Houston—Social
conditions.   3. African Americans—Texas—Houston—Ethnic
identity.   4. Hispanic Americans—Texas—Houston—Ethnic
identity.   5. Houston (Tex.)—Ethnic relations.   6. Houston
(Tex.)—Social conditions.   7. African Americans—Texas—
Houston—Interviews.   8. Hispanic Americans—Texas—
Houston—Interviews.   9. Stereotype (Psychology)—United
States—Case studies.   10. United States—Ethnic relations—Case
studies.   I. Niemann, Yolanda Flores.   II. Rodriguez, Nestor.
III. Title.
F394.H89 N47   2003
305.868′07641411—dc21
2002003439

CONTENTS

*To the memory of my father, Tatcho Mindiola Sr.,
and my brother, Armando Mindiola Sr.*

TATCHO MINDIOLA JR.

*To my husband, Barry Niemann, and our children,
Russell Flores Niemann and Mychaelanne Flores Niemann*

YOLANDA FLORES NIEMANN

To the memory of my father, Domingo G. Rodriguez

NESTOR RODRIGUEZ

List of Tables

PREFACE

The 2000 U.S. Census documented what those who live in urban areas across the United States already know—that the color of America is rapidly changing. One of the most significant forces underlying this change is the dramatic increase in the country's immigrant population, especially Hispanics, over the past three decades, coupled with a moderate increase in the African American population and a much slower increase in the White population.

In the past decade, newspapers and other media predicted that Hispanics would soon become the nation's largest minority group. A prevalent message seemed to be that African American issues would be replaced by those of Hispanics once the latter became the nation's largest minority. Of course, this has not occurred: even as Hispanics have begun to surpass African Americans in numbers, African Americans and their issues remain very much in front of the public. We felt that the constant media attention has contributed to tension between the two groups. In several regions of the United States, this tension is already evident: Hispanics are the majority in some school districts; and African Americans and Hispanics vie for political offices previously occupied by Whites. The tension seems to be exacerbated by the growing numbers of Hispanic immigrants, most of whom have little direct knowledge of or contact with African Americans. As our students and members of the media questioned us about these demographic changes and their implications for Black-Brown relations, we turned to the social science literature for answers.

We found, however, that the study of race relations in the United States is dominated by concern with Black-White relations and that the literature on minority-minority relations, especially Black-Brown relations, is scant at best. We believe that relations among peoples of color will be a central concern in the twenty-first century. We also believe that because African Americans and Hispanics are the two largest racial-ethnic groups and live in proximity in urban areas, they are destined to receive much of the attention from the media, politicians, corporate America, and researchers. Our observations also indicate that conflict, cooperation, and accommodation characterize relations between Hispanics and African Americans, depending on the context.

Relations vary as well according to the specific situation and locale and according to whether interaction is at the group or individual level. At the national level, for example, several prominent civil rights organizations, such as the Rainbow Coalition and the League of United Latin American Citizens, have issued a statement of collaboration in pursuit of a common agenda. At the individual level, however, issues such as competition for resources and status, stereotypes, and cultural differences influence the perceptions and behaviors of Hispanics and African Americans. Our understanding of these intergroup phenomena is hampered by the lack of research on the topic of minority-minority relations. Thus our goal here is to begin to fill the large gap in our knowledge of group relations as they pertain to African Americans and Hispanics. In our analyses, we consider several dimensions of Black-Brown relations.

The demographic dimension speaks to the rapid growth in the Hispanic population. Hispanic immigrants are important actors in this scenario because they are perceived as an economic threat, especially to persons in the lower classes.

The second dimension relates to intergroup perceptions and attitudes. Hispanics and African Americans have preconceived notions about each other. These stereotypes, many of which are negative, seem most prevalent among Hispanic immigrants and females. The role of women in facilitating intergroup relations is a prime focus of our analyses. Thus this work contributes to group relations literature in focusing on an area that has been largely ignored.

Consensus and conflict are yet another dimension of intergroup relations. Our examination of the various issues on which there is agreement and disagreement among African Americans and Hispanics shows that conflict and consensus have important implications for Black-Brown relations.

Cultural differences also have a major impact on the dynamics of intergroup relations in that they are a source of friction and misunderstanding, especially as they relate to language. Spanish is now heard over the airwaves, in the workplace, and on the streets. The spread of the Spanish language has created a backlash among some groups, including African Americans.

Race is also implicated in the dynamics of Black-Brown relations. Although Hispanics and Blacks are referred to as "people of color," thereby setting both groups apart from Whites, they are physically different from each other. There is substantial variation within the Hispanic population, and some Hispanics consider themselves White. However, few African Americans would consider Hispanics White. This difference in perception has implications for Black-Brown relations and for each group's relations with Anglo-Americans.

The final dimension we consider is political efficacy. Hispanics and African Americans are not only competing against Whites for elected and appointed positions, but against each other as well. Hispanics lag behind African Americans in voting power and in the number of elected positions they hold. Yet it seems clear that Hispanics are destined to become the third major political force in the United States, after Whites and African Americans.

Background

The analyses presented in this book reflect our varied interests and scholarship. Each of us is interested in the issues that emanate from race relations, but each of us also has specific interests as they pertain to relations between Hispanics and African Americans. Nestor Rodriguez is interested in immigration from Mexico and other Latin American countries and how this affects relations between Hispanics and African Americans. Yolanda Flores Niemann is interested in stereotypes, women's experiences, and social location and the role they play in Black-Brown relations. Tatcho Mindiola Jr. is interested in the issues that divide African Americans and Hispanics and that foster consensus between them. We consider this work a first effort. Much more needs to be done. We hope it will motivate others to consider how minority-minority relations are changing the dynamics of race relations in the United States.

Terminology

One of the first issues we confronted in writing this volume was how to refer to the groups in question. Both African Americans and Hispanics have a history of using different labels to refer to their own group. "Negro," "Colored," "Afro-American," "African American," and "Black" have been some of the terms used by people of African origin. "Latin

American," "Spanish American," "Hispanic," and "Latino" have been used by Mexicans, Cubans, Puerto Ricans, and others who have a common heritage and culture. Among Mexican-origin people, the terms "Mexican American" and "Chicano" have also been used. We are sensitive to the ideological underpinnings of each term and the controversy that surrounds many of them. We use "Hispanic" in this book not because we approve of or identify with the term but because it is preferred at this time in Houston, Texas. The same reasoning explains our use of the terms "African American," "Black," "Anglo," and "White."

A Note of Thanks

We wish to express our appreciation to the Center for Mexican American Studies at the University of Houston for sponsoring the survey that serves as the foundation of this book. We are also grateful to Adolfo Santos and Luis Salinas of the University of Houston for their statistical advice and assistance. Special thanks are due Maria Gonzales and Ada Vaglienty of the Center for Mexican American Studies for their assistance in constructing the tables and formatting the chapters. We also thank our editor at the University of Texas Press, Theresa May, and the anonymous reviewers who gave us invaluable comments on the manuscript.

BLACK-BROWN RELATIONS AND STEREOTYPES

Chapter 1

Emerging Relations between African Americans and Hispanics

When we start pushing for power, someone's going to have to give it up.

HISPANIC POLITICAL ORGANIZER, HOUSTON, TEXAS
(QUOTED IN *GOVERNING*, JANUARY 1993, 32)

We worked for it, we were beaten, we were spat upon. We'll work with you for it, but do you have to take it from us?

AFRICAN AMERICAN ELECTED OFFICIAL, HOUSTON, TEXAS
(QUOTED IN *GOVERNING*, JANUARY 1993, 32)

African Americans and Hispanics have co-resided in the United States for more than one hundred fifty years, so why have relations between these two populations become a salient topic at the beginning of the twenty-first century? There are several answers to this question. First, by the end of the twentieth century the two populations formed majorities in the largest U.S. urban centers. And the 2000 census showed that together these two groups of color outnumbered non-Hispanic Whites in the largest five U.S. cities (see table 1.1). This had never happened before in U.S. history. Second, there is a greater presence of the two groups across various social settings, for example, neighborhoods, workplaces, public school systems, universities, and social service agencies. This has occurred even in the Deep South, where Hispanics immigrated in large numbers in the 1990s. In Georgia, for example, the number of Hispanics quadrupled to 435,000 between 1990 and 2000 (U.S. Census Bureau 2001b, table 2). As we describe in the following chapters, these changes create opportunities for cooperation, competition, or conflict. A good deal of what social scientists and other urban observers say about

Table 1.1 Racial-Ethnic Group Populations
of the Five Largest U.S. Cities, 2000

	TOTAL POPULATION (IN 1,000S)	NON-HISPANIC WHITE	AFRICAN AMERICAN	HISPANIC	ASIAN	OTHER[a]
New York	8,008[b]	2,801	2,130	2,161	787	1,515
Los Angeles	3,695	1,099	415	1,719	369	1,176
Chicago	2,896	907	1,065	754	126	490
Houston	1,953	602	494	731	104	393
Philadelphia	1,518	644	656	129	68	111

[a] "Other" includes the categories "American Indian and Alaskan Native," "Native Hawaiian and other Pacific Islander," "Some other race," and "Two or more races."
[b] The separate group categories do not sum to the total population because Hispanics may be of any race.

Source: U.S. Census Bureau 2001a, table 4.

social relations in U.S. society in the twenty-first century will concern African Americans and Hispanics.

For much of the history of the social sciences in the United States, the study of intergroup relations has focused primarily on Blacks and Whites. While government agencies such as the U.S. Census Bureau as well as public school systems classify many Hispanics as White, many Hispanics feel this is a misclassification (Sándor 1994). Mexican Americans, Central Americans, Puerto Ricans, Cuban Americans—all of these groups know that in many ways they live in worlds very different from that of European-origin White Americans. According to Delgado (1999), the Black/White binary tends to relegate non-Black minority groups to the background. This has implications for how other minorities are viewed: "The Black/White binary conveys to everyone that there's just one group worth worrying about. . . . Only one group, blacks, has moral standing to demand attention and solicitude" (Delgado 1999, 120). From this perspective, it becomes easy to ignore the social problems faced by Hispanics, and it even justifies restrictive measures against them, such as limiting immigration or deportation of Hispanic husbands and wives and fathers and mothers. In this book, we move Hispanics to center stage in the country's intergroup drama by reviewing evolving issues of Black-Brown relations.

According to the U.S. Census Bureau (1998, table 19), by 2005 Hispanics will outnumber African Americans in the United States. This already occurred in some major U.S. cities (e.g., Los Angeles and Houston) in the 1990s. This development represents a major sociodemographic shift in U.S. society. Even as the two populations have become major social and political actors across many areas of the country, only a few studies (e.g., Cruz 1998; Torres 1995) have attempted to explain or project the emerging patterns of interaction and attitudes between them. The primary concerns in the social sciences continue to be questions of immigrant assimilation and race relations between Whites and Blacks. This book breaks from this tradition and addresses, from a case study perspective, what we consider important issues in relations between African Americans and Hispanics in the United States. It does this from the belief that Black-Brown relations will play an increasingly significant role, if not a critical one, in the social growth of the United States.

Third, African Americans and Hispanics became increasingly important political actors in the United States during the late twentieth century. All five of the largest U.S. cities have now had Black mayors, and Hispanics have won political offices in major metropolitan areas. African Americans and Hispanics have also enjoyed some success in attaining appointments to high positions in public administration. Of course, this Black and Brown political ascendancy contrasts dramatically with earlier years when both groups were politically invisible. For example, it was only about three decades ago that the Houston City Council had no Black or Brown members, and it was only about two decades ago that the Houston City Council had no Hispanic members. Yet the pressing questions of Black-Brown relations do not so much concern which group tallies a greater number of political offices but how their political ascendancy will affect intergroup relations. Will it lead to political alliances based on a shared memory of minority experiences, or will it lead to new levels of intergroup conflict? Of course, African Americans and Hispanics will not remain alone in the country's urban political landscape. Although no longer a numerical majority, Whites will continue to play major if not dominant political roles, sometimes affecting the course of Black-Brown relations.

Both African American and Hispanic political observers have viewed White political interests from the perspective of Black-Brown relations with caution. A southern African American elected official has stated this view as follows: "Blacks and browns have been at odds because we've for the most part been parceled out crumbs from the table, the fatback and the neck bones. When we focus on those we never get to the steak" (quoted in Gurwitt 1993, 36).

The growing numerical dominance of African Americans and Hispanics in large U.S. cities and the recent Hispanic immigration into southern states with large Black populations raise a variety of questions concerning the future of the relations between these two populations. For example, much remains to be learned about social stereotypes and interactional attitudes that Blacks and Hispanics hold of each other. How do African Americans view Hispanic immigrants and their impact on the country's social development? Are Blacks seen by Hispanics as privileged beneficiaries of government programs for minorities? Do Blacks act favorably or unfavorably toward Hispanics? Because Hispanics make up a large proportion of immigrants to the United States, it is necessary to study these questions from the perspectives of both U.S.-born and foreign-born Hispanics. As occurs in any group divided into established residents and new immigrants, the attitudes and social behavior of recently arrived and established Hispanics sometimes differ and are sometimes at odds (Bach 1993).

Houston as a Research Setting

In several ways the Houston area qualifies as an instructive site of African American–Hispanic relations. First, it is the fourth largest U.S. city, whose 742,207 Hispanics and 461,584 Blacks constitute 63 percent of the total population of 1,917,835 (U.S. Census Bureau 2000a, table 1). This is by far the largest total Black and Brown population in a southern urban area. Moreover, Houston has both the largest Black population and the largest Hispanic population of any southern city.

Second, the Houston area is experiencing dynamic demographic changes as a result of immigration. Although Hispanics make up the majority of new immigrants to the Houston area, there are a large number of Asian–Pacific Islanders as well. Unlike other urban areas with a long history of immigration, the Houston area's immigrant influx is fairly recent. In 1970 less than 3 percent of the city's population was foreign born; by the mid-1990s the city's foreign-born population accounted for 23 percent of residents. As we describe in detail later, Hispanic immigration is sometimes considered to have a negative impact on Black-Brown relations because Hispanic immigrants are thought to compete with Blacks for jobs, especially in the lower echelons of the labor market (Briggs 1992).

Third, the Houston area has been the focus of intergroup research for at least ten years, allowing a systematic comparison of attitudinal and behavioral trends over a long period. The major source of this research has been the Houston Area Survey conducted by the sociologist Stephen Klineberg at Rice University. This survey has been conducted annually since 1982 and asks a range of questions regarding intergroup relations, immigration, education, employment, and other issues. Another research source is a survey of intergroup relations conducted by the Tomás Rivera Center in 1993. This survey explored through a random sample of Anglo, African American, and Hispanic respondents perceptions of intergroup relations and of a host of other issues. A key component of the survey was to gauge the quality of intergroup relations in the Houston area. Finally, a random survey was conducted in 1996 by the Center for Mexican American Studies (CMAS) at the University of Houston to investigate intergroup perceptions among African Americans, U.S.-born Hispanics, and foreign-born Hispanics. This survey, described below, serves as the principal data source for the discussion in this book.

The Survey and Sample Characteristics

The 1996 survey was conducted among a sample of 600 African Americans and 600 Hispanics. The survey respondents, eighteen years of age and older, were randomly selected and interviewed through telephone calls in Harris County, the core area of metropolitan Houston. Of the 600 Hispanic respondents, 348 were foreign born and 252 were born in the United States. This allows for a three-way comparison among the African American, U.S.-born Hispanic, and foreign-born Hispanic subsamples. Among the foreign-born Hispanic respondents, the top three nationalities were Mexican (about two-thirds), Salvadoran, and Colombian.

Sixty percent of the sample was female and 40 percent was male. Among African American respondents the median age was thirty-nine, while among the U.S.- and foreign-born Hispanic respondents the median ages were thirty-three and thirty-four, respectively. A large majority of U.S.- and foreign-born Hispanic respondents were married (60 percent and 75 percent, respectively), while 42 percent of the African American respondents were married. Twenty-nine percent of African Americans reported living with someone, and 20 percent reported being divorced or separated; the rates for U.S.-born Hispanics were 22 percent and 12 percent, respectively, and for foreign-born Hispanics 12 percent and 7 percent, respectively. The reported levels of education were 12.3 years among African Americans, 11.7 years among U.S.-born Hispanics, and 8.6 years among foreign-born Hispanics. The occupations reported most frequently by the three respondent groups were professional jobs among African Americans (21 percent), administrative-support jobs among U.S.-born Hispanics (21 percent), and service jobs among foreign-born Hispanics (35 percent). African American and Hispanic respondents reported unemployment rates of 8 percent, while foreign-born Hispanic respondents reported an unemployment rate of 5 percent. The most common political identification among African American and U.S.-born Hispanic respondents was liberal (about one-third of each group), while the most common political identification among foreign-born Hispanic respondents was conservative (about one-third), although one-fourth of African Americans and almost one-third of U.S.-born Hispanics also gave this political identity.

The median household income of the respondents was $29,182 among African Americans, $27,949 among U.S.-born Hispanics, and $18,596 among foreign-born Hispanics. A majority of the three respondent groups reported having households with children in elementary school, though foreign-born Hispanics reported this at a substantially higher rate, 71 percent. More than one-third of all three groups reported having households with children in middle school, and more than one-fourth of all three groups reported having households with children in high school.

Historical Background

Houston's Black-Brown relations in the late twentieth century should be interpreted at least in part from the perspective of their historical antecedents. To understand this background is to understand why questions concerning the future of these intergroup relations can be posed from opposing standpoints. On the one hand, it can be expected that the two groups are headed for confrontation, as they have evolved politically through the hard knocks of racial and ethnic struggles, where racial-ethnic self-interest is the central political value. On the other hand, it can be expected that the two groups are headed for accommodation, as they realize that they can overcome the power of the dominant group only through political cooperation based on a common identity and unity. Both of these perspectives reflect the subordinate origins of the two groups.

Early History

Quite literally, Houston was established through Black-Brown relations. Black slaves and Mexican prisoners captured from Santa Anna's army cleared the swampland on which the city would be built in 1836 (De Leon 1989). According to historical accounts by O. F. Allen, no White man could have endured the insect stings, malaria, snakebites, impure water, and other hardships experienced by those who cleared the land (cited in De Leon 1989, 5). When word reached Texas of Emancipation on June 19, 1865 ("Juneteenth"), about one thousand slaves were in Houston. The African American population increased after Juneteenth as freed slaves migrated to the city in search of work. The 1900 census counted 14,608 Blacks in Houston, about one-third of the city's total population (Shelton et al. 1989). Far fewer Hispanics were counted: only about 1,000 Mexican-origin residents lived in the city at the turn of the century.

While in-migration from surrounding localities promoted Black population growth in Houston, Hispanic population growth was spurred by immigration occasioned by the breakout of the Mexican Revolution in 1910. The 1910s also saw the city's political districts, or wards, begin to take on racial and ethnic boundaries. Blacks concentrated in the Third, Fourth, and Fifth Wards, and Mexicans concentrated in the Second Ward (Feagin 1988). Several factors affected Black-Brown relations as the two populations accommodated themselves in the city. Undoubtedly, previous relationships in rural areas between members of both groups lessened their social distance somewhat. African Americans and Hispanics who migrated to Houston from southern Texas, for example, sometimes came from the same rural communities, where they worked for White landowners and occasionally interacted in community events (e.g., Juneteenth celebrations). In their rural homes individual African Americans and Hispanics sometimes formed close relationships. Yet the closeness of the two groups should not be overemphasized as major factors also kept them apart.

A major divisive factor was the development of Jim Crowism, which affected both groups. Houston was a Confederate city, and its Confederate heritage endured well into the twentieth century. It was the first

Texas city to have a Ku Klux Klan chapter, Sam Houston Klan Number One, which was formed in 1920 (Carleton 1985). The national Klan leadership appointed a former Harris County deputy sheriff its top Klan leader in Texas, with authority to develop Klan chapters throughout the state. The Texas Klan became the most powerful in the South, and it attacked and intimidated Blacks and Mexican Americans alike. In Houston the Klan sometimes served as a parallel "law enforcement" agency as Klan members, some of whom were in fact law enforcement officers, tapped telephone lines, intercepted telegraph messages, and placed spies in post offices (Carleton 1985).

Jim Crowism

Jim Crowism constructed boundaries that separated all groups, not just Whites and Blacks. It created White, Black, and "Mexican" schools, churches, and restaurants. Although Jim Crowism did not mandate segregation of Blacks and Hispanics, it nonetheless promoted it. It promoted the concept that social group life operated on a demarcated sociospatial plane whereby each group had its place and violations were severely if not fatally punished. In Texas Whites, Blacks, and Hispanics — and in Houston, Asians — occupied a multitiered system reminiscent of South African apartheid as Mexican Americans were sometimes allowed more "freedoms" (e.g., seating at the front of the bus) than Blacks.

Segregation created divisions between African Americans and Hispanics in Houston if for no other reason than that it produced rigid residential divisions between the two groups. While racial and ethnic groups often form residential enclaves, segregation reinforced this social separation with the power of law and social mores (Feagin 1988). But White-imposed segregation was not the only thing that kept Blacks and Hispanics apart. While they themselves were restricted from many White-owned places, some Hispanics applied Jim Crow segregation practices to Blacks. A Mexican-owned restaurant chain in the city, for example, denied service to African Americans until the passage of the 1964 Civil Rights Act (De Leon 1989). Hispanic leaders in the city also resisted attempts to have Mexican students segregated with Black students, arguing that Hispanics were "Whites" and thus not subject to Texas's segregation laws (De Leon 1989). This argument was most likely born out of a resistance to the socially stigmatized status of people of color, especially African Americans.

Immigrant Labor and the Urban Labor Market

Undoubtedly, as in other U.S. cities, in the first half of the century African Americans in Houston began to notice labor market group divisions as some employers started to favor immigrant Hispanic workers. The 1920s saw a growing interest in Mexican immigrant labor among rural and urban employers in the United States (Reisler 1976). The Bracero Program, initiated in 1942 to import temporary Mexican laborers as a wartime measure, annually provided hundreds of thousands of Mexican workers to U.S. employers (Craig 1971). While braceros worked mainly in agriculture, a small number were employed in cities. In the Houston area, they laid railroad tracks; the company took special measures to separate them from U.S. workers.

By the end of the 1940s, two-thirds of Hispanics in the Southwest lived in urban areas. In the cities and towns of the Southwest, Hispanic workers became concentrated in low-paying occupations. In Houston these were also the sectors where many African Americans looked for jobs. Over the decades Hispanic workers gained a degree of occupational distribution, while African American workers remained fairly restricted. The 1970 census, for example, found that 45.0 percent of Black workers in the Houston area had service, household domestic, and laborer jobs, whereas 23.2 percent of Hispanic workers had these occupations (U.S. Census Bureau 1972, tables P-6 and P-8). Moreover, a greater proportion of Hispanic workers (15.8 percent) had professional and managerial jobs than did African American workers (10.0 percent). These occupational differences led to disparities in income and poverty rates. The 1970 census found that Hispanic households had an annual median income of $8,218 and a poverty rate of 15.8 percent, whereas African American households had a median income of $6,213 and a poverty rate of 26.8 percent (U.S. Census Bureau 1972, tables P-6 and P-8). In the 1980s and 1990s, however, massive immigration of working-class Hispanics increased the concentration of Hispanics in the lower sectors of the labor market.

Internal Hispanic Division and McCarthyism

In the political arena, Houston Hispanic leaders were divided at midcentury on how Hispanics should react to African Americans' efforts to end segregation. Some favored working with the NAACP, while others leaders felt this alliance would only serve to antagonize Whites and further distance them from Hispanics (De Leon 1989). Some Hispanic leaders in the Houston area felt that a common minority status required a united front against discrimination, while others felt that working with Blacks against racism was to admit that Hispanics were less than White. The question of whether to work with Blacks against segregation or to work separately divided two prominent figures in the League of United Latin American Citizens, a national Hispanic organization (De Leon 1989).

It should be pointed out that in the 1950s a political perception among Houston Whites acted to further isolate African Americans in a way that it did not similarly affect Hispanics. Just as Houston became a Jim Crow stronghold in the first part of the century, it became a hotbed of right-wing extremism in the 1950s, which culminated in the city becoming a major center of McCarthyism. Indeed, it was in Houston that Senator Joseph McCarthy made one of his last speeches (celebrating Texas independence from Mexico) before he was debunked on national television (Carleton 1985). McCarthyism in Houston created a large and active network of anticommunist groups who considered any change in the established social order subversive. For many members of these groups, including Houston's power elite, communism, labor unions, and the civil rights movement were seen as the same threat. Attempts by the federal government and liberal groups to end school segregation, for example, were seen by ultraconservatives as attacks against individual freedom and the coming of "one-world" government and socialism. So entrenched were the ultraconservatives in their philosophy of free enterprise and nongovernment involvement that their elected representatives on the Houston school board forbade school cafeterias from using federally inspected meats and from providing free federal breakfast programs for indigent students, many of whom were Black and Hispanic (Carleton 1985). The Houston police spied on progressives who worked with Black groups on the grounds that this meant they had "Communist tendencies."

The Black and Chicano Movements

The Black and Chicano social movements of the 1960s and 1970s created a new level of Black-Brown relations in the Houston area. The two movements represented a wide range of goals and perceptions rather than a united political thrust within each group. Some activists in the two movements perceived their goal as the attainment of equal rights in U.S.

society, while others sought to do away with the White power structure. At various levels opportunities arose for political collaboration among movement activists. Members of both groups supported each other ideologically and sometimes cooperated in political work. For example, in one case an African American and a Chicano running for political office campaigned for each other in precincts where the other had a constituency. In some cases, African American and Chicano university students came together to participate in protests. In addition to fostering political coalitions, the Black and Chicano movements promoted a shared view among many African Americans and Chicanos that people of color in the United States had a common enemy and thus a common stake in struggles to transform U.S. society. Indeed, the perception of the need for collective activism extended to popular struggles in the peripheral countries of the capitalist world system. Long after the Black and Chicano movements subsided, the perception of the need for intergroup political solidarity remained a value for many African Americans and Chicanos. However, stereotypes and competition for resources, among other factors, have mediated this solidarity.

New Social Developments

In several ways the period of the mid-1970s and the mid-1980s represents a watershed in Houston's development and in relations between African Americans and Hispanics in the Houston area. It was an interval that saw its oil-based economy swing from record-setting growth to a steep recession that brought a loss of more than two hundred thousand jobs (Shelton et al. 1989). Two developments during this time particularly affected relations between African Americans and Hispanics. One was a massive Hispanic immigration, which started in the mid-1970s and accelerated in the 1980s and into the 1990s. Another was the emergence of Africans Americans and Hispanics into significant political power bases with a growing ability to influence institutional change across the city. Both developments had consequences for Black-Brown relations well into the 1990s.

Immigration

The 1980 census counted 116,084 Hispanic immigrants in the Houston metropolitan area, more than 40 percent of whom had immigrated in the previous five years (U.S. Census Bureau 1983, table 195). In the city of Houston, immigrants helped to increase the number of Hispanics to

281,000, almost two-thirds of the African American population. In 1990 the census found that the number of Hispanic immigrants in the Houston metropolitan area had grown to 274,000 (U.S. Census Bureau 1993, table 28) and that in the city of Houston the Hispanic population had grown to 450,000, only 8,000 fewer than the number of African Americans. This difference was more than made up by the large number of uncounted, undocumented Hispanic immigrants in the city. The impact of immigration on Hispanic population growth by the 1990 census had been dramatic; 44 percent of Hispanics in the city were foreign born, compared to just 3 percent of Blacks. By 2000 approximately half of all Hispanics in the city were foreign born, while the proportion of foreign born remained low among Blacks.

Among the most significant ways that the massive influx of Hispanic immigrants affected Black-Brown relations in Houston are the following: (1) it increased the size of the Hispanic population so that it equaled the Black population; (2) it helped to create common residential areas for Blacks and Browns; (3) it introduced a new group into the labor market; and (4) it introduced cultural change, including the use of Spanish. The consequences of Hispanic immigration for Black-Brown relations cannot be overstated. Given their numerical equality, many Hispanics now expected equal representation with African Americans in appointments to public office and institutional settings. For example, as immigration helped to swell the Hispanic student population in the Houston Independent School District (HISD), Hispanics looked forward to the appointment of a Hispanic school superintendent. Hispanics also expected greater political representation. African Americans became the point of reference for many Hispanics to measure their political progress in the Houston area. To be sure, this was mainly a perception among established Hispanic residents, not among new immigrants.

Hispanic immigration helped to create common residential areas for African Americans and Hispanics in two ways. First, the new immigrant settlement zones in the city's southwestern sector quickly attracted other low-income residents. It is ironic that many new Hispanic immigrants, especially Central Americans, arrived in the city as the economy entered a steep recession that created a major housing opportunity for them and for other low-income residents. Before the area's economic downturn began in 1982–1983, apartments and new homes for middle- and high-income earners were being built at a record-setting pace (Feagin 1988). When the recession developed and thousands of unemployed office workers left the city, the rental housing industry entered into a crisis. Thousands of apartment units in the city's predominantly White southwestern area stood empty because the middle-income renter population was decimated and because developers had built an oversupply of apartments in the late 1970s and early 1980s. Apartment owners and managers hit on a dramatic temporary solution to the crisis—enticing Hispanic immigrant renters. For many apartment owners and managers this could only be a temporary solution, since profits fell sharply as rents were reduced by more than half for the new population of low-income Hispanic immigrants.

As apartment owners and managers attracted new Hispanic immigrants with low rents and ethnic amenities, including changing the names of apartment buildings to Spanish, other low-income renters (e.g., African Americans) also moved into the city's southwestern area. This Black-Brown residential development was a major shift out of the established racial and ethnic residential wards in the eastern half of the city. Especially in the southwestern sector, more African Americans and Hispanics shared common residential areas than ever before in the city's history. Of course, the introduction of tens of thousands of African American and Hispanic residents into the city's western areas, which were heavily White until the late 1970s, was also historically significant.

The second way in which immigration created common residential areas involved the settlement of new Hispanic immigrants in African American wards near the city's downtown. By the late 1980s a small number of Hispanic immigrant households settled in the African American Fourth Ward, and by the late 1990s Hispanic immigrants accounted for an increasingly visible percentage of Fourth Ward residents. Hispanic growth in the Fourth Ward stopped in the late 1990s, however, when the area was redeveloped for downtown office workers. Hispanic immigrants also moved into the African American Third Ward just southwest of downtown, but the number of immigrant households was relatively small and most of this new settlement occurred at the edges of the ward. Other established African American residential areas near downtown also saw the encroachment of Hispanic immigrant households. In some cases, immigration expanded and established Hispanic settlement zones to the very edges of African American neighborhoods. This created substantial overlap of social spaces (health clinics, public parks, shopping centers, etc.) used by the two groups. In surrounding public schools, the Black-Brown overlap sometimes led to racial conflict.

Immigration has contributed substantially to the workforce in the

Houston area, especially in the lower echelons of the labor market, where historically Blacks had outnumbered Hispanics. As recently as the 1980 census there were more Black than Hispanic domestic workers and laborers in the city (U.S. Census Bureau 1983, tables P-15 and P-21), but by the 1990 census the reverse was true (U.S. Census Bureau 1993, table 185). It is doubtful that this comparative occupational shift can be explained entirely by upward occupational mobility among African Americans. While the proportion of Blacks working in the higher-echelon managerial, professional, technical, and administrative support occupations grew by 10 percent between 1980 and 1990 (U.S. Census Bureau 1983, table P-15; 1993, table 23), a relatively large number (14.7 percent) of African Americans were unemployed in 1990 and a large proportion (27.8 percent) of Black families lived in poverty. These statistics strongly suggest that African Americans faced significant competition from Hispanics in the lower echelons of the city's labor market.

In many labor-intensive industries, employers sought out Hispanic immigrant workers, amounting to reserved labor markets. Soon African American and U.S.-born Hispanic workers stopped looking for work in sectors "reserved" for immigrant labor. It is safe to assume that for some employers racial preference also played a role in this shift from employing Black workers to employing Hispanic immigrant workers. That is, some employers viewed Hispanic workers more favorably than Black workers for racial and cultural reasons, among them that Hispanic immigrants could be hired more cheaply than African Americans, further exacerbating intergroup competition. This may have played a significant part in the transformation of the city's private household workforce of maids and servants from majority Black in 1980 to majority Hispanic in 1990 (U.S. Census Bureau 1993, table 195).

Hispanic immigration also introduced language change in the Houston area, adding to the social distance between African Americans and Hispanics. While individuals and coworkers can find ways to communicate across linguistic boundaries, language difference can create a significant social divide between groups, limiting intergroup interaction mainly to the fringes. When members of linguistically different groups come into close contact, frustrations and tensions can surface in exigent situations. This has characterized intergroup relations for many Hispanic immigrants in Houston who seek medical assistance at public hospitals and clinics where African American personnel screen for patient eligibility. When the latter are slow to act because of language problems, some Hispanic patients take this to mean indifference to or dislike of them. African Americans in turn may experience frustration because they see the introduction of Spanish as an additional barrier to economic mobility. In the words of an African American bank employee in Houston who was turned down for a promotion to the bank's International Department, "At first they wouldn't hire us because we are Black. Now they won't promote us because we don't speak Spanish." The increase in resources for bilingual education, including salaries for bilingual teachers, can also create tensions for African American educators who see an equal or greater need among African American students who were born in this country.

African American and Hispanic Political Development

The late 1970s and the 1980s also mark a political transition period for African Americans and Hispanics in the city of Houston. During this time, many Black and Hispanic leaders turned their attention from the civil rights movement to mainstream politics. To be sure, this transition was not only about race and ethnicity, for in 1981 it also saw the election of the city's first woman mayor, after a long history of good-old-boy politics. The election of Blacks and Hispanics to the city council, the HISD board, and the state legislature became more common, in part as a result of a change in the electoral system from at-large to district representatives. An African American was elected at-large to the city council in 1979, but a Hispanic was not elected at-large for another fifteen years. The at-large election of a Hispanic female to the city council in the mid-1990s marked the first time a Hispanic had won a citywide election since a Hispanic male was elected city controller in the early 1970s. It is also in this political transitional interval that more than one Hispanic was elected to serve on the school board of HISD, which oversaw one of the largest school systems in the country. The defeat in the early 1990s of a mayoral candidate who served as mayor in the 1960s and early 1970s and the election of the city's first Black mayor in the late 1990s indicated that the city's political structure had shifted dramatically. African Americans and Hispanics had become political players.

The process of political maturation in the 1980s was not equal for African Americans and Hispanics, however. Almost all African American adults in Houston were U.S. citizens and thus eligible to vote, while by the early 1990s the majority of Hispanic adults were immigrants, only about one-fifth of whom had obtained U.S. citizenship. Eligible African American voters thus significantly outnumbered eligible Hispanic voters in the city. This fact was not lost on non-Hispanic White political candidates, who campaigned vigorously in African American areas but often slighted Hispanic areas (Rodriguez et al. 1994). Not surprisingly, this candidate apathy was more pronounced in immigrant neighborhoods adjacent to downtown. Yet U.S.-born residents in these established Hispanic areas often accounted for 50 percent or more of the adult population. While Hispanics did not have the numbers to go head-to-head against another voting group, they did have the numbers to make a difference in a close election. This is exactly what happened in 1991 when Hispanic voters gave strong support to a White male opponent of the incumbent female mayor because they felt she was indifferent to their concerns. A majority of Hispanic voters again sided with the White male candidate in a close runoff election against a strong African American candidate. When the White candidate won, some key Hispanic leaders felt Hispanics had entered a new political age. But this perception quickly dissipated, as the core Hispanic political leadership never developed a unified view with respect to Black-Brown political relations. In 1997 a large percentage of Hispanic voters supported the election of the city's first Black mayor.

For the most part, Houston has not experienced the sharp Black-Brown rifts that have been reported in other communities. Johnson, Farrell, and Guinn (1997), for example, describe tension between African Americans and Hispanics in the Los Angeles suburb of Compton spurred by the increase in Hispanic immigration. Some African Americans in Compton see Hispanics as usurpers of public benefits that were won by years of struggle, while some Hispanics see the more politically powerful African American community as a dominant group that discriminates against them. Johnson and colleagues (1997) contend that this Black-Brown conflict in the Los Angeles area is indicative of what will occur in other urban centers in the United States.

In Houston, the predicted Black-Brown conflict materialized in the 1990s in the sphere of educational politics. When a White superintendent resigned from HISD to relocate to another state, many Hispanics expected that a Hispanic candidate would at least be considered for the position. This expectation was based on the fact that the school system's student body was becoming predominantly Hispanic. When the school board met in a closed session and selected one of its own, an African American male, as the new superintendent, many Hispanics in the city felt that the selection process had unfairly excluded consideration of Hispanic candidates. A group of Hispanic leaders attempted to block the selection through court action but were unsuccessful. For weeks African American and Hispanic leaders used the media to accuse each other of unfair treatment. A prominent African American accused Hispanic leaders of conducting a political lynching of the newly selected Black superintendent. The event demonstrated not only how empowered African American and Hispanic leaders in Houston could clash dramatically over an issue but also how a third major actor—Whites—could affect Black-Brown relations. White school board members played a central role in organizing the process that led to the selection of the African American superintendent; moreover, it is almost certain that the White-dominated power elite in the Houston area played a critical role in the decision as well, since they closely oversee various operations of the school system.

In December 2001 Houston's first African American mayor, Lee Brown, faced a heated runoff election to win a third term. The other candidate in the runoff was Orlando Sanchez, a Cuban American city council member. It seemed a classic political standoff between African American and Hispanic voters. Political advertisements in support of Brown dotted African American neighborhoods, just as advertisements in support of Sanchez appeared throughout Hispanic neighborhoods. In the days leading to the election, prominent national political figures endorsed both candidates as polls showed that the election was too close to call. National news media converged on Houston to report what many thought would be the first victory of a Hispanic over a Black in a mayoral race in one of the country's largest cities. Brown pulled off a victory, with support from 96 percent of Black voters, while Sanchez received 66 percent of the Hispanic vote. Yet for all the intergroup interest that the media generated, the election did not develop into a Black versus Hispanic conflict. Although Black and Hispanic voters heavily supported the candidate of their own group, the established Mexican American political leaders divided mainly along party lines, as liberals tended to support Brown, a Democrat, and conservatives tended to support Sanchez, a conservative Republican.

Conclusion

The 2000 census showed that for the first time Hispanics outnumbered African Americans in Houston (U.S. Census Bureau 2001a, table 4). Immigration contributed significantly to this Hispanic population growth, but it also limited Hispanic political ascendance vis-à-vis African Americans. Although the foreign-born rate among Hispanic adults in Houston approached 60 percent in the late 1990s, most Hispanic immigrant adults had not been naturalized and thus did not contribute to the city's Hispanic electoral strength. Indeed, for many Hispanic immigrants, political concerns remained focused on their homelands or on federal immigration policies. The 1990s also saw a division of the Hispanic political center in Houston as some Mexican American leaders were indicted (and two convicted) of bribery and other Mexican American leaders broke ranks with established Mexican American political networks. The city's Hispanic political leadership diversified further when non–Mexican American Hispanics started to enter the political scene. This Hispanic political division and diversification occurred as African Americans appeared to reach a political apex in Houston. The election and appointments of African Americans in Houston to several key offices, including the mayor's office and a congressional seat, demonstrated that African Americans had arrived politically, even if the White power elite still exerted considerable and at times decisive institutional influence.

The political sphere, of course, does not determine the totality of Black-Brown relations. Indeed, the political posturing of African American and Hispanic leaders does not always represent the sentiments of common residents in their communities (Romo and Rodriguez 1993). The priorities of African American and Hispanic political leaders who seek benefits for their own groups may vary considerably from the priorities of common Black and Brown residents who reach across racial and ethnic boundaries for common survival as neighbors or as coworkers. All social spheres (community, educational, religious, work, etc.) contain opportunities to promote or limit intergroup relations and how this works out often depends on the exigency of the moment. This is not to say that the actions of key institutional leaders do not create broad intergroup impacts, for they do. The course of Black-Brown relations in Houston at the beginning of the new century depends significantly on whether African American and Hispanic leaders continue to play racial-ethnic politics or move into a new political phase of greater Black-Brown unity. But the future course of Black-Brown relations in Houston, as elsewhere in the country, will also depend significantly on how African American and Hispanic residents perceive and interact in their everyday lives.

Chapter 2

Stereotypes and Their Implications for Intergroup Relations

You go by what you hear or what is portrayed in the media like what we see on TV. Hispanics are still portrayed as wetbacks coming over the border.

THIRTY-FIVE-YEAR-OLD
AFRICAN AMERICAN WOMAN

In Mexico we don't see many Black people, except in movies, and they're always bad people in movies. I'm afraid of Black people.

THIRTY-ONE-YEAR-OLD MEXICAN-BORN WOMAN

Stereotypes are pictures in our heads about a category of people (Lippmann 1922). More specifically, stereotypes are positive or negative sets of beliefs held by an individual about the characteristics of a group. These beliefs vary in their accuracy. For example, a common stereotype about Hispanics is that they are uneducated. Indeed, only about 11 percent of Hispanics over twenty-five years of age have college degrees, according to the 2000 U.S. Census. In the Black-Brown survey sample, the median educational level of Hispanics is ten years compared to twelve years for African Americans. In general, the educational attainment level of Hispanics is among the lowest of any group in the United States. Therefore, in this case it is statistically accurate to say that the group as a whole is undereducated. Stereotypes also vary in terms of the extent to which they capture the traits they describe. To take the example above, the stereotype that Hispanics are not educated is inaccurate at least for the 11 percent of this population who have received college degrees and for the increasing number of Hispanics who are currently pursuing a college education.

Stereotypes also vary in the extent to which the beliefs are shared by others (Jones 1997). For instance, in largely agricultural communities, most Hispanics may be migrant workers. As a result, a stereotype may develop that Hispanics in general work as migrant agricultural laborers. In industrial communities, there may be different stereotypes of Hispanics and labor. Stereotypes affect emotional reactions to other ethnic-racial groups. The stereotype that African Americans are criminally inclined may elicit fear; women may clutch their purses when African American men pass by.

Stereotypes also shape expectancies and perceptions and lead to exaggeration of group differences (Jussim, McCauley, and Lee 1995); influence our judgment of and behavior toward a person; and produce generalizations about group members (Jones 1997). When Hispanics and African Americans apply for jobs, for example, interviews and job qualifications may be perceived through the lens of the stereotype, leading to biased and unfair judgments.

Stereotypes generally tend to be negative (Niemann 1999, 2000; Niemann et al. 1994), suggesting that they are used not just to simplify the world but also to justify discrimination against and hostility toward the out-group (Peffley and Hurwitz 1998, 61). The insidious nature of stereotypes lies in part in that they may be activated consciously or unconsciously (Devine 1989). "It is not an overstatement to argue that stereotypes are destructive forces that historically have evolved punitive and discriminatory responses to ethnic, racial and religious groups" (Peffley and Hurwitz 1998, 61). Indeed, social psychologists consider stereotypes the engine that drives prejudice (Jones 1997).

The Generation and Maintenance of Intergroup Stereotypes

Stereotypes that are found in day-to-day perceptions and attitudes are generated and maintained by a complex set of forces, including racism, social ecological context, legitimizing history texts, the media, and social science research. Through these forces stereotypes have become embedded in the collective consciousness of society.

Stereotypes and Racism

Stereotypes justify racism. Throughout U.S. history, politically and economically powerful forces have sought to represent members of various ethnic-racial groups in a manner that suits their agendas. This representation has institutionalized and rationalized a racial hierarchy that defines "superior" groups as "justifiably" dominant and "inferior" groups as deserving their status in society. Most Americans are indoctrinated in some version of this racist ideology from their earliest years (Feagin 2000). "This ideology includes an extensive system of myths, prejudices, and stereotypes that is continually reproduced, legitimized, and disseminated through the mass media, schools, workplaces, legislatures, and churches" (Feagin 2000, 32). Thus stereotypes cannot be separated from the historical framework of structural, institutional, and societal racism in the United States (Feagin 2000, 106). Regardless of the circumstances under which they may have been generated, because stereotypes are embedded in the national and individual consciousness, they are very difficult to change (Fiske and Taylor 1991).

In many ways the relationship between stereotypes and racism is subtler today than it was fifty years ago. For example, most of us can agree that the enslavement of Black Americans, the enactment of Jim Crow laws, the segregation of Hispanics and African Americans, and Whites' belief in their superiority were all a function of racism. Today, however, overtly racist behavior is no longer socially or politically sanctioned.

Research documents that most individuals in the United States think of themselves as fair-minded, certainly not as racist. Group stereotypes make it relatively easy for individuals to blame members of disadvantaged racial groups for their predicaments and their relatively lower place in the social hierarchy. To the casual observer, stereotypes seem to have a kernel of truth; that is, they are based on apparently objective observation of these groups (Jussim, McCauley, and Lee 1995; Oakes, Haslam, and Turner 1994). If racism is a shameful thing of the past, then people must be solely to blame for their predicaments in the present. It is hard for many people to accept that economic, educational, health care, and workplace disparities between Whites and African Americans and Hispanics are related to societal stereotypes and covert or institutionalized racism (Niemann and Secord 1995).

For example, lack of higher educational achievement is a major concern for Hispanics and African Americans. However, in many communities they are "tracked" into vocational programs. By definition, these programs do not prepare students for college. Yet such race-based tracking is justified by some educators from their stereotypical belief that these minority children are not going to college anyway, so why subject them to the challenges of the more difficult classes? This treatment of students facilitates low rates of college-educated Hispanics and African Americans and contributes to the stereotype that they are uneducated.

Group stereotypes also make it acceptable to use racially loaded language. Such language includes referring to African American women as welfare mothers, to Hispanic women as baby makers, to African American and Hispanic men as criminals, and to Hispanics as illegal aliens. Although racial slurs are unacceptable in public, such terms as "nigger," "alien," "wetback," and "illegal" often guide everyday thinking and behavior (Feagin 2000). The prevalence and the acceptance of stereotypes thus not only affect social structures and their formal roles, they also affect private behavior and language.

Stereotypes and Social Ecologies

Stereotypes are neither categorically true nor categorically false (Helmreich 1997; Niemann and Secord 1995; Oakes, Haslam, and Turner 1994). When people think in stereotypical terms, they express such views as "Blacks play basketball" or "Hispanics are maids and gardeners." These statements convey the sentiment that Blacks and Hispanics have *inherent* traits that make them good basketball players and maids or gardeners. However, while it may be true that they often engage in these activities, the underlying reasons for this have to do with societal, contextual factors and not with inherent traits.

The social ecological approach to stereotypes (McArthur and Baron 1983; Niemann and Secord 1995) stipulates that in-group and out-group perceptions of complex, community-wide behaviors and situations form the bases for the generation and maintenance of stereotypes. Behaviors that are repeated and perceived as sanctioned by and within a given ethnic community may become stereotypes that are accepted within ethnic groups and by out-group observers, in large part because they appear to reflect social reality. Perceivers associate the context itself, and related behaviors, as inherent to these groups (Niemann and Secord 1995) rather than as resulting from current and historical treatment of them (Niemann et al. 1998). The manner in which people are perceived is so context-dependent that groups are seen categorically in a manner consistent with the contexts in which they are typically observed. The stereotypical traits thus seem true and become part of consensual societal knowledge. Cultural models consider society itself the basis of stored knowledge, and stereotypes are seen as public information about social groups that is shared among the individuals within a culture. In this approach, although stereotypes exist "in the head[s] of the society's perceivers," they exist also in the "fabric of the society" itself (Stangor and Shaller 2000, 68).

For example, it is the case that Hispanics have one of the highest drop-out rates in the United States. Those who think of Hispanics as not being academically oriented believe that it has to do with their inherent intelligence or motivation. But they fail to consider the social ecological factors that contribute to what some Hispanic activists refer to as a school "push-out" rate. These factors include language barriers, poverty, and institutional racism in educational settings. Similarly, it is true that African American and Hispanic men are overrepresented in the criminal justice system relative to their numbers in the general population. This statistic is often used to talk about an inherent criminality without taking into consideration the social ecological factors that contribute to the situation. These factors include overpolicing of minority neighborhoods, a biased criminal justice system, and racial profiling, three issues that are receiving national attention.

Institutionalized racial segregation that has resulted in separate White and minority communities contributes to the stereotype that African Americans and Hispanics do not care enough to live in areas that afford a higher quality of life because of "the kind of people they are." The casual observer typically is unaware of discriminatory policies such as redlining that keep ethnic-racial minorities out of predominantly White neighborhoods, which typically have higher tax bases and hence good services and a higher quality of life, including water drainage, garbage disposal, police protection, and high-quality schools. Because of continuing racism and de facto segregation, such neighborhoods are stereotypically associated with White values.

In many urban areas, Hispanic immigrant men stand on street corners waiting to be hired as day laborers. This behavior contributes to the stereotype that they are not responsible enough to obtain "regular jobs." The unaware observer fails to understand the many obstacles these men face as they try to obtain jobs that employ their skills—obstacles that are usually embedded in their status as undocumented immigrants. Similarly, the widespread hiring of Hispanic women as household servants contributes to the stereotype that Hispanic women prefer this work and are particularly suited for it—a common racist ideology used by employers to justify hiring women in low-paying positions (Hossfeld 1994; Segura 1994).

The lack of understanding of the role of context is related to lack of contact between racial-ethnic groups. Under conditions of equal status, contact between different groups improves understanding and knowledge (Gaertner et al. 1994). However, because of the way in which groups are situated and perceived, intergroup contact sometimes reinforces stereotypes. In urban areas with large Hispanic populations, Hispanics are more likely than other racial-ethnic group members to work in custodial occupations. Having contact with Hispanics in this role may serve to confirm the stereotype that Hispanics are inherently suited for this type of work. In addition, there are power differences between the persons who have the resources to hire Hispanic custodians and maids and those they are hiring. Because it is human nature to justify privileged positions, this power difference can serve to confirm the stereotype that Hispanics are less deserving of power and status. Unfortunately, "[w]hen we condemn stereotypes, it is always other people's, almost never our own! We are happy to assume that our own stereotypes are valid even as we reject others' stereotypes as false" (Oakes, Haslam, and Turner 1994, 206).

To promote positive relations between African and Hispanics, group leaders must help their constituents to understand the relationship between stereotypes and the social inequities that underlie the contexts in which the groups are situated and perceived. African Americans must pay attention to the manner in which many Hispanics, especially foreign-born immigrants, are denied civil rights. Hispanics must understand the effect of overt and covert racism and power differences between racial groups on the everyday experiences of African Americans. An understanding that social hierarchies underlie stereotype-consistent contexts will facilitate relations between the groups.

Stereotypes and Legitimizing History

One reason that Americans are largely unaware of the contexts that underlie stereotypes is that history texts continue to underplay, deny, or ignore the impact of racism on the experiences of African Americans and Hispanics today. History texts leave the reader with the impression that the current status of groups is a function of group members' inherent traits and behaviors, thereby generating and maintaining stereotypes.

For instance, history texts remain largely silent regarding how the dehumanization and enslavement of African Americans continues to benefit White Americans while continuing to harm African Americans. Few texts discuss the continuing role of racism in producing group disparities in the crucial areas of education, health, housing, employment, and credit. Texts typically mention the *Brown v. Board of Education* ruling that set the stage for racial integration in schools. However, they do not point out that school segregation continued decades after the ruling and that White flight to the suburbs in part reflects resistance to integration. Texts do not speculate about the effects on Black children of White adults and children continuing to fight integration.

With respect to Hispanics, there is virtually no discussion in history texts of the political maneuverings that led to U.S. colonization and subsequent ownership of the five southwestern states that were once Mexican territory. Yet these same texts portray Mexican workers in the United States as "illegals" or "aliens" who are taxing educational and medical institutions. Most texts do not discuss how Mexican immigrants have been denied basic civil rights while being used to fill critical labor needs. In general, there has been little acknowledgment of the Hispanic presence in the United States and the role of Hispanics in shaping U.S. history. In fact, recent analyses of history books have often referred to Hispanics with terms such as "the invisible minority" or "the emerging minority."

History texts generally do not discuss events that could facilitate understanding between Hispanics and African Americans. They do not mention that the battle of the Alamo was fought in large part over slavery: White newcomers to Texas wanted the right to own slaves, while slavery had been outlawed in Mexico. Loewen writes, "The Alamo lies deep in the heart of (White) Texans; woe to any textbook that might point out that love of slavery motivated Anglos to fight there for 'freedom'" (1995, 273).

In general, history books legitimize myths that benefit the existing social hierarchy while giving scant attention to the role of racism in establishing and maintaining the hierarchy. Only 40 percent of the textbooks examined by Loewen list racism, racial prejudice, or any term beginning with *race* in their indexes (Loewen 1995). The forces that determine the content of history books and thus the content of U.S. history will not allow portrayals that challenge existing myths and the hierarchical status quo. Thus the legitimizing myths and images portrayed in history books both create and reflect societal thought and stereotypes.

An accurate representation of U.S. history that includes critical analyses of the role of racism in the past and current experiences of today's Hispanics and African Americans would contribute greatly to the diffusion and changing of group stereotypes. Teachers can help students to focus on the larger picture, including the effects of colonization and laws and policies that have different effects on ethnic-racial groups (Loewen 1995). In addition, teaching history backward from the present can help students to understand the impact of past and current policies on today's realities (Loewen 1995). Finally, history texts that encompass all of history can help students to understand that they have the power to diminish the continuing inequities in society and their effects on intergroup perceptions, especially negative group stereotypes.

Stereotypes and Social Science Research

Social science research of the mid-twentieth century laid the foundation for current literature on stereotypes. This early literature at various times described African Americans as lazy, childlike, unable to take care of themselves, irresponsible, having out of control sexual drives, militant, victims, and creators and members of a culture of poverty. The few positive stereotypes have related to musical and athletic skills. Hispanic men have been described as respectful, family oriented, hardworking, interested in mechanical training, beer drinkers, dancers, boxers, musical, and being skilled in "the art of rapidly drawing, opening, and slashing with a pocket knife" (Humphrey 1945, 72; see also Niemann 2001). Hispanic women have been described either as home centered, submissive, docile, respectful, and modest in dress and behavior or as rebellious, "independent, free moving women" (Humphrey 1945, 75; Niemann 2001). Hispanic men and women have been stereotyped as possessing low moral standards; as thieves; as dirty; as helping to keep wages low; as spreaders of disease; as lazy and shiftless; as artistic; and as ignorant and inferior (Niemann 2001; Richards 1950).

Until the last decade, most social scientists who wrote about Hispanics and African Americans were typically outside observers completely unfamiliar with the peoples or cultures they were studying. Nevertheless, their work has become part of the societal "knowledge" about Hispanics and African Americans. This flawed research is also passed on to graduate and undergraduate students. Furthermore, in many social science programs, the curriculum does not expose students to cultural differences between groups, thereby perpetuating stereotypes. Such an incomplete curriculum is damaging, as college students are the nation's future corporate leaders, politicians, psychologists, and other professionals.

Some social science organizations, such as the American Psychological Association, recently have attempted to address the lack of cultural education by mandating that graduate programs include culturally sensitive literature in their curricula.

Stereotypes and Competition for Resources

Competition for resources and status may also serve to generate and maintain group stereotypes (Jones 1997). Fear of competition may underlie policies dealing with welfare, crime, affirmative action, and immigration (Peffley and Hurwitz 1998). Many Hispanics believe that government policies created to help minorities primarily benefit African Americans. Hispanic university faculty in general believe that affirmative action has served African American colleagues more than it has served Hispanics. Consequently, Hispanic faculty indicate less support for affirmative action policies than do their African American counterparts (Niemann and Dovidio 1998). These political stands, in turn, affect race relations.

On the other hand, Black Americans feel a sense of entitlement to some community institutions because of the struggles that took place in the 1960s to establish them. Many believe that Hispanics have benefited from their hard-fought battles for civil rights (Guevara 1996; Johnson and Oliver 1994). In California, "Hispanics, particularly undocumented, are seen as free-riders, gaining all the benefits of such public services as the local public hospital without having paid the price to get them in the community" (Johnson and Oliver 1994, 200). These attitudes are related to competition for status within the racial hierarchy of U.S. society. Such attitudes are not limited to California. In other areas of the United States, Black-Brown relations are conditioned by situations in which these two groups compete, such as housing and economic restructuring, and by the policy demands of Black and Hispanic political representatives on behalf of their constituencies (Guevara 1996).

The limited research on relations between African Americans and Hispanics indicates that interethnic conflict is a new configuration of group conflict in urban America. Conflict seems to be precipitated by a combination of economic forces, social dislocations such as Hispanics taking over previously Black-occupied housing areas, and changing demographics (Johnson and Oliver 1994). As long as the Hispanic population was small, competition between Blacks and Browns was muted. Now, however, when Hispanics equal African Americans in numbers, issues that lead to competition have been brought into sharper focus. For example, social dislocation of low-income African Americans is exacerbated by increasing immigration from Mexico, a growing penetration by newly arriving immigrant groups into formerly all-Black residential and business areas, and by increasing competition for scarce and valued resources (Johnson and Oliver 1994). These conditions underlie Black-Brown conflict in geographic areas where the concentrations of both groups are high.

Research based in California, as well as our research, shows that Blacks strongly believe that undocumented Mexicans take jobs from American citizens (Johnson and Oliver 1994). Blacks also believe that once a Hispanic family moves into an apartment building, it rapidly becomes all Hispanic, leading to residential displacement of Blacks. At the same time, many Blacks also believe that Mexicans and Hispanics are displacing them from traditionally Black residential areas and business opportunities (Johnson and Oliver 1994).

Stereotypes and the Media

The media are a particularly powerful force in generating and maintaining stereotypes of Hispanics and African Americans (Duck, Hogg, and Terry 2000). Influential media genres include novels, newspapers, film, television, and advertising. Early portrayals of African American men as dangerous to young White women (e.g., *Birth of a Nation*) and of African American women as "mammies" are images that are still prevalent in marketing campaigns today (Feagin 2000). Portrayals of Hispanics have included "the Frito Bandito," the lazy Mexican taking a siesta, and images of bad, seductive women who seek to take good White men from good White women (Cortés 1997). In the last decade, there has been some attempt in television programming to improve the images of African Americans. Interestingly, movie images have lately situated African Americans in "magical," healing roles (e.g., *The Green Mile*) or in Black-White police partner roles (e.g., *Lethal Weapon*). However, Hispanics are rarely portrayed in television dramas, situation comedies, or movies. Indeed, they are virtually invisible in television and cinema. While the media have helped to shape negative stereotypes of African Americans and Hispanics, they are doing little to reverse or diffuse them.

Often the media are the primary or only source of information about Hispanics and African Americans. In many areas of the country, communities are prominently White. There is little or no contact with people of color. Indeed, in predominantly White states such as Washington it is not unusual for college students to report that the first time they were in proximity to a Hispanic or an African American person was in the first few weeks of college. Media images are particularly powerful for groups who lack contact with each other. When people do have personal contact with members of other groups, their interpretations of behaviors are shaped by the stereotypical images depicted in the media. Media images become the lens through which African Americans and Hispanics are viewed.

As a major conveyor of cultural knowledge, the mass media play a significant role in imparting behavioral information that results from contexts associated with racism, for example, high dropout and incarceration rates. However, the media do not undertake to explain the role race plays in situating groups in contexts that lead to negative or risky behavior. By making race a seemingly invisible and irrelevant force in Hispanics' and African Americans' experiences, the media contribute significantly to the stereotype that negative contexts are inherently associated with racial-ethnic minority groups (Duck, Hogg, and Terry 2000; Jones 1997).

Media portrayal is considered so important to the experiences of Hispanics and African Americans that groups that represent them, such as the National Council of La Raza and the NAACP, have called for major changes in the portrayal of minorities on television. They have vowed to monitor media portrayals, or the lack thereof, and to put pressure on the media to produce fair portrayals.

African Americans on Hispanics and Hispanics on African Americans

The limited research that exists on Black-Brown relations shows that Hispanics and African Americans hold many negative stereotypes about each other (Niemann et al. 1994). A random sample of Hispanic and African American college respondents were asked to list traits that characterize the other group. The ten most frequently used terms are presented in table 2.1 (see also Niemann et al. 1994). Although the list includes both positive and negative traits, Hispanics express more negative views about African Americans than vice versa (Niemann et al. 1994).

In describing Hispanic males, Blacks used five positive terms—hard workers, pleasant, caring, attractive, and intelligent; three negative terms —antagonistic, lower class, and alcohol users; and two neutral, physically descriptive terms—short and dark hair. In describing Black males, His-

Table 2.1 College Respondent Stereotypes

Hispanics about Black Males		Hispanics about Black Females	
Athletic	Criminal	Speak loudly	Dark skin
Antagonistic	Tall	Athletic	Antagonistic
Pleasant	Dark skin	Egotistical	Fashion-conscious
Speak loudly	Unmannerly	Unmannerly	Lower-class
Muscular	Sociable	Sociable	Ambitionless

Blacks about Hispanic Males		Blacks about Hispanic Females	
Antagonistic	Alcohol users	Family-oriented	Lower-class
Hard worker	Short	Determined	Caring
Pleasant	Dark hair	Pleasant	Passive
Caring	Attractive	Dark hair	Short
Lower-class	Intelligent	Attractive	Long hair

panics used three positive terms—athletic, pleasant, and sociable; four negative terms—antagonistic, speak loudly, criminal, and unmannerly; and three neutral, physically descriptive terms—muscular, tall, and dark skin.

Blacks described Hispanic women in positive or neutral terms, including attractive, family oriented, and determined; "passive" was the only negative descriptor. Conversely, Hispanics perceived Black women in mostly negative terms—speak loudly, egotistical, unmannerly, antagonistic, and lacking ambition; positive terms included athletic, sociable, and fashion-conscious.

Although the results in the 1994 study by Niemann and colleagues are consistent with other research on stereotyping, most of this body of work has been conducted with college student populations. This research sample can be problematic, because the identities of college students are still being shaped and their experiences, independent from their families, are limited (Sears 1986). Therefore, it may not be possible to generalize the results from the existing research to minority group, noncollege populations. In the 1994 study we conjectured that a more accurate picture of intergroup stereotypes might be obtained from the responses of members of the community-at-large. However, we found that college student stereotypes are very similar to those of the population at large, as discussed below.

Community Study of Black-Brown Stereotypes

The goals of the community stereotype research reported here were to investigate the stereotypes that African Americans and Hispanics have of each other, to examine the meaning of the stereotypes, and to examine the relationship between the groups and group stereotypes. The respondents were asked to give three words or phrases that they thought described African Americans and Hispanics. This method reveals the traits or phrases that are part of the respondents' consciousness and reality.[1]

Table 2.2 lists the thirty most frequent terms that African Americans and U.S.- and foreign-born Hispanics provided about each other in the survey.[2] The majority of traits are consistent with previous stereotype-content research with student respondents (e.g., Niemann et al. 1994; Niemann, O'Connor, and McLorie 1998). For example, terms that U.S.- and foreign-born Hispanics used to describe African Americans included noisy/loud, hostile, athletic, aggressive, angry, poor, welfare recipient, and violent. These terms are consistent with findings from much of the research on African American stereotypes (Niemann et al. 1998). Terms that African Americans used to describe Hispanics are also consistent with previous research and include hardworking, family oriented, poor English, dropouts, lazy, illegal, Spanish-speaking (Niemann 1999). This overlap speaks to the pervasiveness of consensual stereotypes that shape societal beliefs and perceptions. As a Black respondent stated,

> Black people are no different from any other group in this country; they watch too much TV. The media is where most of the ideas about Hispanics are generated. We watch the news and see people trying to cross the borders and we heard about people coming here to work. The stories we see are negative and we are socialized to believe that these people are bad.

New Stereotypes?

In the present research, all respondents were African American or Hispanic, nonstudent community members. It is important to pay attention to terms that distinguish this research from other work as they may be the most predictive of current and future interethnic group relations.

Unique traits provided by respondents in the survey are listed in

Table 2.2 Top 30 Terms Used to Describe African Americans and Hispanics in Order of Frequency

AFRICAN AMERICAN TARGETS		HISPANIC TARGETS
Traits Provided by U.S.-Born Hispanics	*Traits Provided by Foreign-Born Hispanics*	*Traits Provided by African Americans*
Good people	Good people	Hardworking
Friendly/nice	Friendly/nice	Friendly/nice
Hardworking	Hardworking	United
Oppressed	Oppressed	Good people
Noisy/loud	Noisy/loud	Family oriented
Lazy	Cultural identity	Considerate/fair
Cultural identity	Lazy	Cultural identity
Dropouts/uneducated	Dropouts/uneducated	Oppressed
United	United	Growing population
Diverse	Hostile	Poor English
Hostile	Diverse	Intelligent
Considerate/fair	Considerate/fair	Religious
Complainers/whiners	Complainers/whiners	Honest
Athletic	Have Progressed	Poor (economically)
Have Progressed	Athletic	Opportunistic
Strong-minded	Bad people	Underpaid
Bad people	Strong-minded	Dropouts/uneducated
Prejudiced	Family oriented	Playful/fun-loving
Complacent/passive	Aggressive	Education oriented
Aggressive	Prejudiced	Have progressed
Family oriented	Complacent/passive	Proud
Angry	Talented	Aggressive
Talented	Religious	Taking over jobs
Religious	Poor (economically)	Strong-minded
Disrespectful/rude	Easygoing	Hostile
Poor	Disrespectful/rude	Illegal
Easygoing	Angry	Diverse
Misunderstood	History-minded	Lazy
Welfare recipient	Welfare recipient	Spanish-speaking
Violent	Misunderstood	Attractive

Table 2.3 Respondents' Views of Members of the Other Group

HISPANICS ABOUT AFRICAN AMERICANS		AFRICAN AMERICANS ABOUT HISPANICS	
Family-oriented	Hardworking	Oppressed	Intelligent
Good people	Friendly	Opportunistic	Playful/fun-loving
Prejudiced	Religious	Education oriented	Proud
Easygoing	United	Aggressive	Taking over jobs
Bad people	Considerate/fair	Strong-minded	Growing population
Complainers	Disrespectful/rude	Underpaid	

table 2.3. Several of the terms describing Hispanics deal with competition, for example, taking over jobs, underpaid, growing population, opportunistic. These issues are discussed in chapters 3 and 5 and are consistent with other research that shows that negative beliefs or feelings that African Americans have about Hispanics may be grounded in competition for resources (Guevara 1996; Johnson and Oliver 1994). A twenty-eight-year-old Black male expressed this sentiment:

> I see how these Mexicans have run down these jobs. They come in and they do jobs for the minimum amount of money and in turn it runs down the pay scales for the jobs.

Another respondent, a twenty-year-old Black female, said,

> I'm getting paid to take care of my business and I'm tired of giving all my money to welfare, and basically, the Mexican and Hispanics are the ones that are on welfare.

Hispanics' beliefs and feelings about African Americans may also be grounded in competition. A thirty-five-year-old Hispanic male said,

> Government policies only care about Black people. Blacks get the nice, government office jobs, while our people are still working in the fields picking apples. Blacks don't seem to care that they are treated better than we are.

Group Consensus

Importantly, as seen in table 2.1, some of the most frequent descriptors that Hispanics and African Americans provided about each other are indicative of the perception of common humanity between the groups. Shared intergroup traits were as follows (in alphabetical order):

aggressive	friendly/nice	poor
considerate/fair	good people	have progressed
cultural identity	hardworking	religious
diverse	hostile	strong-minded
family oriented	oppressed	united

The list above is interesting because of its implications for group unity. African Americans and Hispanics believe, among other things, that their communities are hostile. Indeed, of the fifteen terms, only "hostile" is negative. What is unknown is toward whom the groups believe the hostility is directed—each other, the dominant group, or society in general? What are the circumstances of their hostility? Can hostility be used as a starting point for closer relations?

Perceptions of hostility are overwhelmed by more positive views. Both groups see themselves as aggressive but also fair, friendly, good, and hardworking. They also see themselves as religious, strong-minded, and united (in their own communities). African Americans and Hispanics also describe themselves as diverse and family oriented. These stereotypes are reflected in the following quotations.

> I think Hispanics are a much closer people than Blacks are; they work together and Blacks could learn a lot from them by helping family members. Because they always stick together, they know how to save money; . . . five, six, seven of them live in a house together and they aren't worried about who is doing this and who is doing that, like Blacks always do.
>
> FORTY-ONE-YEAR-OLD BLACK RESPONDENT

> Blacks and Hispanics are similar because we're both at the bottom of the barrel.
>
> TWENTY-YEAR-OLD BLACK FEMALE

Are Stereotypes Positive or Negative?

Language carries cultural knowledge. In American culture, for instance, the word "aggressive" may be seen as a positive trait for men but not for women. In other cultures, "aggressive" may be associated with negative cultural attributes, such as lack of respect. It cannot be assumed that we know the meanings that people assign to descriptive terms. Knowledge of stereotype-content descriptors is not enough information to ascertain intergroup attitudes. What is also needed is the meanings respondents assign to on each trait (Esses, Haddock, and Zanna 1993; Niemann and Jennings 1995). Therefore, in the Black-Brown study, after the respondents listed three descriptive traits, they were asked to indicate how favorable each trait was by ranking it on a scale from 1 to 5, with 5 being the most positive.

Results indicate that in general African Americans have more positive views of Hispanics than vice versa. These findings are consistent with previous research, as discussed earlier. Specifically, African Americans rated 68 percent of terms they provided about Hispanics as positive and only 25 percent as negative. Two of the examples of the positive manner in which African Americans perceive Hispanics are provided below.

> Hispanic people remind me of the way Black people used to be. Family is important, children are special, and elders are revered. Hispanic families seem to be foundations on which to grow; it seems no matter what they face they stay strong and persevere.

> We don't unite as much as Hispanic people would. Hispanic people take jobs and work more seriously, not on all levels, but for the most part more than Black people do.

In contrast, U.S.-born Hispanics rated 52 percent of the terms about African Americans as positive compared to 43 percent by foreign-born Hispanics. U.S.-born Hispanics rated 38 percent of terms about African Americans as negative compared to 47 percent by foreign-born Hispanics. These differences are reflected in the following statements.

> I work with Black people and I went to high school with them. They have some different ways, but you see how they're discriminated against just like we are. Once you get to know them you know they're not like what you thought or what the media portrays—all criminals and using crack.
>
> Forty-two-year-old U.S.-born Hispanic male

> I just don't trust them and don't want them around my kids. The men, especially, all use drugs and they all carry guns; and the

women are so loud. I've seen that on TV and I just don't want to have to be around them, so I avoid them.

THIRTY-NINE-YEAR-OLD MEXICAN-BORN FEMALE

Clearly Hispanics hold more negative terms about African Americans, and within the Hispanic community the foreign born do so more than the U.S. born (see chap. 3).

Ethnic Group Collective Esteem and Intergroup Relations

Research has found that the more negative people feel about their own group, the more negative they feel about another group. And the converse is true: the more positive people feel about their group, the more positive they feel about another group. Social psychologists inform us that people have two aspects of identity—personal and social (Tajfel 1969; Tajfel and Turner 1986). Social identity is related to the groups that we belong to, for example, social clubs and schools. Based on the extent to which we have a strong collective ethnic identity, we may protect that identity in the face of threat by denigrating others (Crocker and Luhtanen 1990; Tajfel and Turner 1986). Do these findings hold true when we compare African Americans and Hispanics? Could feelings about collective identity explain African Americans' more positive intergroup stereotypes compared to those of Hispanics? To answer these questions it is important to understand the relationship between African Americans' and Hispanics' feelings about their own and each other's ethnic-racial group. This relationship may have important implications for intervention. For instance, if a relationship is found between negative ethnic esteem and negative beliefs about out-groups, intervention may begin by focusing on in-group esteem. If there is no relationship, intervention may focus directly on intergroup issues.

To examine this relationship, we asked respondents the extent to which they agreed (on a scale of 1 to 5) with the following five questions taken from a widely used collective self-esteem scale (Crocker and Luhtanen 1990):[3] (1) I am a worthy member of my racial-ethnic group; (2) I often regret that I belong to my racial-ethnic group; (3) Overall, my racial-ethnic group is considered good by others; (4) In general, I'm glad to be a member of my racial-ethnic group; and (5) Most people consider my racial-ethnic group, on the average, to be more ineffective than other racial-ethnic groups.

Results indicated that of the five items, the only one that predicted whether respondents believed a stereotype trait was positive or negative was the private ethnic esteem item, "I often regret that I belong to my ethnic group." The item was significantly predictive of U.S.-born and foreign-born Hispanics' positivity ratings of traits they provided for African Americans. The results indicate that for Hispanics, the stronger their disagreement with the item, the more positive their trait rating. That is, there seems to be a strong and positive correlation between Hispanics' pride in their ethnic group and their positive perception of African Americans. However, the correlation does not apply for African Americans' perceptions of Hispanics.

Findings

Differences between U.S.-born and Foreign-born Hispanics

There are no substantial differences between U.S.-born and foreign-born Hispanics on stereotype content about African Americans. The two groups agreed on twenty-nine of the top thirty traits that each group provided about African Americans. Not only did they use the same descriptors, but the order of frequency was similar. However, there are differences between U.S.-born and foreign-born Hispanics in positive and negative feelings attached to stereotypes, with the foreign born holding more negative interpretations. The foreign born may have more negative perceptions because they believe that race relations in the United States is a Black/White issue. Foreign-born Hispanics may believe that compared to African Americans they are ignored with respect to civil rights issues. They may believe that only African Americans are deemed worthy of fair treatment, while the foreign born continue to be scapegoats for economic downturns in the United States.

Latino scholars argue that the structure of antidiscrimination law is dichotomous, assuming that one is either Black or White — the Black/White binary described by Delgado (1999). Such an assumption works against Latinos who make claims of racial discrimination. This assumption works even more strongly against Hispanic immigrants. That is, not only are they not Black, they are not American. Hispanic immigrants feel acutely the pain of what they perceive as lack of civil rights protection, especially in comparison to African Americans (Niemann et al. 1999). The foreign born may believe that African Americans are no longer victims of discrimination, especially compared to that experienced by Mexican immigrants. Thus they may believe that negative stereotypes about African

Americans are a function of inherent laziness, criminality, and so on, and not the result of lack of opportunities often experienced by Mexican immigrants. The U.S. born, on the other hand, have had a greater opportunity to observe discrimination against themselves and African Americans. They may feel an affinity with African Americans because of common experiences of oppression in the United States.

Another explanation for the difference in U.S-born and foreign-born perceptions and attitudes may be the significant differences in their experiences (Gurin, Hurtado, and Peng 1994). These distinctions vary in relation to length of residence, language facility, geographic dispersal, contact, and likelihood of working in ethnically diverse settings. In other words, macrosocial conditions set up microsocial conditions that influence social identities and roles that generate stereotype content (Gurin, Hurtado, and Peng 1994). For instance, lack of fluency in English may position Hispanic immigrants at the bottom of the workplace structure. The lower status of foreign-born Hispanics, relative to both African Americans and U.S.-born Hispanics, may affect how they perceive African Americans.

U.S.- and foreign-born Hispanics also have different patterns of intragroup and intergroup contacts, with the former having more contact with members of other ethnic groups than with foreign-born persons of Mexican descent (Gurin, Hurtado, and Peng 1994). This contact allows for knowledge of the heterogeneity within groups. In other words, if Hispanic immigrants have little information about African Americans and if they have very few occasions to interact with them, the only behaviors they will know about are those that attract media attention (Leyens, Yzerbyt, and Schadron 1994). Since stereotype content may be shaped by consensual societal beliefs, it may differ between those persons born in the United States and those born elsewhere, who have had differential exposure to societal beliefs. Contact level may therefore result in a different picture of African Americans for foreign-born than for U.S.-born Hispanics.

Consistency with Previous Research

Examination of intergroup stereotypes reveals that each group holds a complex view of the other that includes positive and negative stereotypes as well as that both groups have stereotypes in common. Results indicate that intergroup perceptions may be grounded in competition for resources and status and in differences in values (e.g., Guevara 1996;

Oliver and Johnson 1994). For instance, it is commonly believed by African Americans that Hispanics take jobs from them. These findings are consistent with ours (see chap. 5). On the other hand, Hispanics' stereotypes of African Americans seem to be more grounded in differences in values, for example, that they are "family oriented."

Group Esteem and Stereotypes

Results also indicate that ethnic group esteem is predictive of Hispanics' attitudes toward African Americans. Recall that the more Hispanics disagree with the item "I often regret that I belong to my ethnic group," the more positively they perceive African Americans. This finding is consistent with other research that shows low group esteem is related to denigration of others (Phinney 1990, 1991). That is, the higher the opinion of one's own group, the more positive one's perception will be of other groups.

However, the same predictive relationship does not hold true for African Americans. Results showed no relationship between African Americans' perceptions of their own group and their perceptions of Hispanics. Why? It could be that for African Americans, whose history of oppression can be traced to their arrival in this country, denigrating groups on the basis of racial identity is considered more of a taboo than is the case for members of other groups. However, it may also be that African Americans are not as threatened by their collective, ethnic social identities as are Hispanics. It could be that they are more accustomed than Hispanics to the knowledge that they are stigmatized by others. This is especially true for foreign-born persons of Mexican descent, who come from a country in which their group is the majority. The stigmatization they experience in the United States, even if it was expected, is new and acutely felt and thus is more threatening to collective ethnic esteem than it is for African Americans. In addition, because collective ethnic esteem is largely affected by group members' perceptions of their status in a given context, African Americans' perception of their group status may be enhanced by their relatively greater participation in city and state government (Guevara 1996). In any event, it is important to note that there was also no negative relationship between African Americans' collective group esteem and their perceptions of Hispanics. That is, the results for African Americans were neutral.

Therefore, a focus on Hispanics' and African Americans' positive ingroup identity that serves to raise the perception of their group without denigrating each other's group may facilitate positive intergroup relations. Such a focus would include awareness of the ways in which the groups have survived extreme oppression, such as slavery for Blacks and denial of civil rights for Hispanics who have been used as a source of cheap labor, as well as awareness of more recent, subtler forms of racism, such as movements against affirmative action and bilingual education. This focus would also include celebration of how Hispanics and African Americans continue to shape U.S. culture.

An example of the relationship between in-group and out-group perception is that college students who pursue ethnic or multicultural studies generally exhibit greater acceptance of differences between groups. This acceptance decreases or eliminates feelings of hostility based on group membership (Blaine 2000; Niemann n.d.). Intergroup acceptance is related to subscribing to moral norms, especially those within a group (Manstead 2000). If Hispanics and African Americans focus on collective group esteem that includes inculcation of attitudes of acceptance and moral treatment of each other's group, those attitudes will then be related to positive behaviors consistent with the group's prototypical moral norms (Terry, Hogg, and White 2000).

Heterogeneity of Groups

Accurate and current information on Black-Brown stereotype content may provide community leaders with clues for reducing conflict and enhancing group relations. Leaders may focus on perceived group commonalities to shape common-group identities among African Americans and Hispanics. This new merged identity would be in addition to individual ethnic-racial group identities (Dovidio, Gaertner, and Validzic 1998; Gaertner et al. 2000). If some of the content traits indicate a common predicament for both groups (Sherif 1966), leaders may focus on these to forge group unity, reduce conflict, enhance relations, and move toward political progress beneficial to both groups. Information on stereotype content can also shed light on the basis for misperceptions and misinformation.

A goal of this book is to suggest research- and theory-based solutions that lead to enhancing intergroup relations between Hispanics and African Americans. We have already identified some ways in which knowledge of stereotypes may be used toward this end, but the research on stereotypes tells us much more. When group members' ethnic-racial identity is salient in a given interaction, the stereotype of their group is likely to be applied to them, especially in the absence of individuating information. This generalization happens even though most of us intuitively and cognitively realize that all members of a group cannot possibly be the same. Nevertheless, we perceive members of our own ethnic-racial group as relatively more heterogeneous in comparison to the perceived homogeneity of members of out-groups (Simon and Brown 2000).

This out-group homogeneity effect is a major lesson from decades of stereotype research. We suggest here that one of the ways in which to improve relations between Hispanics and African Americans is for community leaders to help their group members understand the heterogeneity of each group. We believe that this approach will be much more effective than the more common approach of demonstrating the falseness of group stereotypes. Leaders can help their group members to understand that stereotypes and traits they believe are inherent to out-group members are grounded in how those groups are situated in society. Furthermore, within a group, members are situated differently, in terms of education and socioeconomic status, for example. In that sense, group members need to understand that stereotypes are fluid, variable, and context-dependent.

Generalized change in stereotypes occurs with increased complexity of intergroup perceptions. Therefore, awareness of the heterogeneity of out-groups will have four specific positive consequences. First, we will be less likely to stereotype all group members as one type (Hewstone 2000). Second, we are more likely to see out-group members as being as differentiated as are members of our own group. Third, we will be more likely to work with each other. Fourth and perhaps most important, understanding of heterogeneity will not only reduce overall stereotyping but also will likely make us more amenable to understanding the situated contexts that result from past and current oppression and discrimination of African and Hispanic Americans.

Notes

1. The study presented here employed free response methodology to examine stereotypes of the African American, U.S.-born Hispanic, and foreign-born Hispanic community and to inquire about the meaning of the terms for respondents. This method differs from traditional methodologies, which are generally assessed with trait checklists (e.g., Katz and Braly 1933). In the checklist method, respondents are presented with a list of traits and asked to indicate whether each trait applies to a specific group. Respondents therefore are encouraged to think about the application of terms or traits that may not have been part of their own cognitive set of stereotypes. However, free responses assess respondents' own cognitive set and thus represent stereotypes more accurately than do checklists (Niemann et al. 1994).

2. Coding of these free responses proceeded as follows. First, all descriptions were listed. Second, a five-member research team determined which terms were synonymous (e.g., strong-minded = strong-willed; disrespectful = rude). Third, each unique term and its synonyms were assigned a number, or code, resulting in a master code. Fourth, all responses were coded according to the master code. Frequencies of descriptors were then tabulated.

3. The items from the Collective Self-Esteem Scale are

   A. I am a worthy member of my racial-ethnic group.
   B. I often regret that I belong to my racial-ethnic group.
   C. Overall, my racial-ethnic group is considered good by others.
   D. In general, I'm glad to be a member of my racial-ethnic group.
   E. Most people consider my racial-ethnic group, on the average, to be more ineffective than other racial-ethnic groups.

   Results of regression analyses indicated that the item "I often regret that I belong to my racial-ethnic group" was significantly predictive of U.S.-born Hispanics' ratings of traits they provided for African Americans, $\beta = .27, p < .05$, and of foreign-born Hispanics' ratings of traits they provided for African Americans, $\beta = .25, p < .001$. The Beta values indicate that the direction of association is positive. That is, the stronger the disagreement with the item "I often regret that I belong to my ethnic group" (this item was reverse scored), the more positive the trait rating.

   Results of correlation analyses indicated that the item was significantly predictive of U.S.-born Hispanics' ratings of traits they provided for African Americans, $\beta = .27, p < .05$, and of foreign-born Hispanics' ratings of traits they provided for African Americans, $\beta = .25, p < .001$. The Beta values indicate that the direction of association is positive. That is, the stronger the disagreement with the item "I often regret that I belong to my ethnic group" (this item was reverse scored), the more positive the trait rating.

Chapter 3

Areas of Disagreement

There is conflict and competition and fighting and all of that because we are all scrambling over each other trying to get somewhere.

THIRTY-FIVE-YEAR-OLD U.S.-BORN HISPANIC FEMALE

Blacks and Browns have to work on our differences and come together to form a permanent and history-making coalition. We have to talk about it, write about it, dream about it, and make it happen, because if we don't, the powers that be are going to keep us divided and prevent us from realizing our common destinies of justice and fairness.

TWENTY-SEVEN-YEAR-OLD AFRICAN AMERICAN MALE

Disagreements between ethnic groups in the United States are not unknown. There has been conflict between Scots and Irish and Germans and Italians and between Whites and most people of color. Disagreements also exist between Blacks and Jews, Asians and Blacks, and, as this chapter illustrates, between Hispanics and Blacks.

Our discussion in this chapter is drawn from the Black-Brown survey conducted in Houston in 1996 and from interviews carried out over the past ten years among African Americans and Hispanics in Houston. The interviews highlight some major findings of the survey and allow the participants to speak for themselves.

The rapid increase in the number of Hispanics in Houston creates the impression among many people, including African Americans, of being overwhelmed. Hispanics are now seen everywhere in the city, as workers, shoppers, and residents. Areas of the city that were predominantly White thirty years ago are now Hispanic enclaves.

Hispanics are significant contributors and competitors in the economy

Table 3.1 Index of Dissimilarity, Harris County, 1990

GROUPS COMPARED	INDEX %
Hispanic/Non-Hispanic Black	59
U.S.-born Hispanic/Non-Hispanic Black	59
Foreign-born Hispanic/Non-Hispanic Black	60

Note: Distribution to foreign-born, native status for tracts with fewer than 400 Hispanics is assumed to be constant 38.9% foreign, the average for these tracts.

Sources: Data are from STF3A (from Census Web site). Foreign-born distribution is from U.S Bureau of the Census 1993, table 28.

and the political and social life of the city. Competition can and often does lead to conflict as groups put their interests above those of others.

Physical and Social Space in Houston

Historically, Hispanics and African Americans have not lived in the same areas of Houston. As Anglos began to leave the inner city for the suburbs in the 1970s, African Americans began to move in. They were joined by Hispanics, who not only moved into former Anglo areas, but into African American neighborhoods as well (Purser 1992). The result is that in Houston Hispanics and African Americans are moderately integrated residentially. The index of dissimilarity, a measure of residential segregation, shows that 59 percent of either Hispanics or African Americans in 1990 would have to move into the other's neighborhoods in order for there to be complete residential integration (table 3.1). Preliminary figures from the 2000 census indicate that the index is 53 percent, meaning that residential integration of Hispanics and African Americans increased during the decade.

Yet the primary setting of interaction between Hispanics and Blacks is not the neighborhood but the workplace (table 3.2). Neighborhoods rank a distant second. In the workplace, interaction may be required to accomplish tasks. But there is also an increased probability of informal interaction, simply because the opportunity presents itself.

Hispanic immigrants live among African Americans to the same degree as U.S.-born Hispanics, but they report considerably less interaction (table 3.3). Approximately 46 percent of Hispanic immigrants in the

Black-Brown survey say they never, or almost never, have any interaction with African Americans, compared to 15 percent of U.S.-born Hispanics. Language differences and workplaces that tend to hire immigrants exclusively explain, in part, low levels of contact and interaction (Rodriguez 1996). U.S.-born Hispanics, because of their more frequent interaction with African Americans and their relative familiarity with both groups, become mediators between foreign-born Hispanics and African Americans. This occurs in workplaces common to all three groups and in the broader society, where U.S.-born Hispanics are involved as never before in protecting the rights of immigrants. Prominent Hispanic organizations involved in immigrant issues are the League of United Latin Ameri-

Table 3.2 Settings of Intergroup Interaction

SETTING	AFRICAN AMERICAN INTERACTION WITH HISPANICS (%)	AFRICAN AMERICAN INTERACTION WITH U.S.-BORN HISPANICS (%)	AFRICAN AMERICAN INTERACTION WITH FOREIGN-BORN HISPANICS (%)
Work	58	61	58
Neighborhood	25	19	21
School	7	10	6
Other places	10	10	15

Table 3.3 Frequency of Interaction between African Americans and U.S.- and Foreign-born Hispanics

FREQUENCY	AFRICAN AMERICAN INTERACTION WITH HISPANICS (%)	AFRICAN AMERICAN INTERACTION WITH U.S.-BORN HISPANICS (%)	AFRICAN AMERICAN INTERACTION WITH FOREIGN-BORN HISPANICS (%)
Frequently	72	63	34
Sometimes	16	22	20
Almost never	6	6	25
Never	6	8	21

Table 3.4 Social Distance between African Americans
and U.S.- and Foreign-born Hispanics

| | % YES | | |
	AFRICAN AMERICANS	U.S.-BORN HISPANICS	FOREIGN-BORN HISPANICS
Would you be willing to:			
work alongside, in the office, or in close contact with (Hispanic/African American)?	96	95	90
live in a neighborhood where a few families are (Hispanic/African American)?	96	91	80
approve of your children having a/an (Hispanic/African American) as a friend?	91	93	87
live next door to a/an (Hispanic/African American)?	91	89	91
live in a neighborhood where half or more of the families are (Hispanic/African American)?	73	63	64
approve of your children having the majority of their friends be (Hispanic/African American)?	63	63	57
send your children to a school that is predominantly (Hispanic/African American)?	62	57	59
approve of your children dating an (Hispanic/African American)?	62	54	46
approve of your children marrying a/an (Hispanic/African American)?	59	47	42

can Citizens (LULAC), the National Council of La Raza (NCLR), and the Mexican American Legal Defense and Educational Fund (MALDEF).

The social distance between African Americans and Hispanic immigrants is illustrated in table 3.4, which lists the responses in the Black-Brown survey to a series of questions dealing with Black-Brown interaction. The respondents were asked if they were willing to interact with members of the other group in a variety of situations, starting with the workplace and moving toward more intimate relations involving dating and marriage.

Generally, the closer the relationship, the less approval it receives from each of the subsamples in the survey. Thus dating and marrying a member of the other group, the most intimate of all relationships, are the least accepted scenarios. However, African Americans are more tolerant of interracial dating and intermarriage than are Hispanics, especially Hispanic immigrants, who show the lowest level of approval. African Americans who tend to approve of interracial dating and intermarriage are young males who have relatively higher incomes and who report frequent interaction with Hispanics. Hispanic immigrants who disapprove of dating and intermarriage tend to be older females who, like many immigrants, never or hardly ever have contact with African Americans.

In summary, the picture that emerges is one of frequent contact between U.S.-born Hispanics and African Americans. In contrast, Hispanic immigrants live among African Americans to the same degree as native-born Hispanics but their contact and interaction is limited given that most immigrants are monolingual Spanish speakers and African Americans are monolingual English speakers. Obviously, these linguistic differences restrict interaction. Hispanic immigrants also state that they are less willing to accept African Americans if it involves intimate relations. This is not surprising given their low levels of contact and linguistic barriers.

Policy Issues

The Black-Brown survey found two patterns of disagreement: one in which African Americans have different views from U.S.- and foreign-born Hispanics and one in which foreign-born Hispanics have a view that differs from that shared by U.S.-born Hispanics and African Americans.

African Americans versus U.S.-born and Foreign-born Hispanics

Government Programs

An issue that engenders disagreement among minority groups is the extent to which the government is helping all minorities obtain equal opportunity. Many minorities believe that the government favors the African American population because of their history, the civil rights movement, and presumed White guilt (*Black/Hispanic Dialogue* 1990). Thus in the Black-Brown survey 50 percent of U.S.-born and 58 percent

Table 3.5 Responses by Ethnic Groups to Selected Questions

	% AGREE		
	U.S.-BORN HISPANICS	FOREIGN-BORN HISPANICS	AFRICAN AMERICANS
Most government programs that are designated for minorities favor African Americans.	50	58	24
Immigrants take jobs from African Americans.	25	13	54
It is okay for people to speak Spanish in the workplace.	75	85	49
Abortion should remain legal in the United States.	46	32	54
Children who work should turn their money over to their parents.	33	58	26
In Houston today there is much conflict between Hispanics and African Americans.	46	45	59
Most African Americans are prejudiced against Hispanics.	32	53	22
Hispanics fear African Americans.	26	43	21
African Americans have too much power.	41	23	3

of foreign-born Hispanics agree that most government programs that are designed for minorities favor African Americans (table 3.5). The following quotations reflect these sentiments.

The government programs that have been implemented for minority equalization or equal opportunity are aimed specifically at the Black community because of the civil rights movement. Higher authorities, decisions makers, policy makers, a percentage of whom are Black, have a Black perspective, not a Hispanic's perspective.

TWENTY-ONE-YEAR-OLD U.S.-BORN HISPANIC MALE

I see it [government preference for African Americans] mostly in job opportunities. Blacks yell a lot that they are discriminated against, that they were once slaves, that the country owes them something because they are Black. I can give you examples, the Metro bus system, Head Start programs, the city and county hospitals. These are all public entities that are controlled by Blacks and they use it to their advantage. Take Metro. They have thousands of employees and most of them are Black. We see it everywhere we go in the city and county. Blacks don't understand that the civil rights laws were made for everyone.

FORTY-THREE-YEAR-OLD U.S.-BORN HISPANIC MALE

African Americans disagree with these sentiments. We found in the Black-Brown survey that approximately 76 percent of respondents said they do not think government programs favor them. The following comments by two African American males are illustrative.

No, they [the government] don't favor anyone. Basically there's been a breakdown in communications. I've talked to some Hispanic people who said that they feel that Blacks are getting everything, getting more out of the struggle, and so they feel left out and ignored. And you have some Blacks saying they got to fight for theirs just like we fought for ours, but basically, we're fighting over who's in the worst condition. But the government, they don't favor one group over another.

THIRTY-SEVEN-YEAR-OLD AFRICAN AMERICAN MALE

I don't think that anyone is being favored. The new demographic realities show that we are moving toward a community that is in fact strongly triethnic, Anglo, African American, and Hispanic. So I don't see favoritism. Competition yes, but favoritism no.

SIXTY-YEAR-OLD AFRICAN AMERICAN MALE

The issue of who is favored by government programs could become moot as federal, state, and local agencies reevaluate affirmative action. In California and Washington State, for example, affirmative action programs based on race and gender have been eliminated. In Texas, affirmative action programs designed to increase the number of Mexican and African Americans in institutions of higher education have been ruled unconstitutional. Recently, however, there are signs that affirmative action may not be dismantled easily. In 1996 Houston voters agreed that the city's affirmative action programs should continue. Also, the University of California system has begun to place more emphasis on the scores of the Scholastic Aptitude Test (SAT) II, which tests knowledge in a particular subject area as opposed to the more general verbal and mathematical reasoning measured by SAT I. Many Hispanic students are taking the SAT II test in Spanish and thereby gaining admission to schools in the University of California system. Critics argue that the University of California has simply set up another affirmative action program to replace those that were declared unconstitutional. It is too early to predict how these changes will affect Hispanic perceptions that African Americans receive affirmative action preference.

Immigration

Hispanic immigration is a major point of contention between Hispanics and African Americans, not only in Houston, but in all the major cities of the country where African American and Hispanic immigrants reside in significant numbers. In Houston, a majority of African Americans believe that the overall effect of immigration is bad (Mindiola et al. 1996) because immigrants take their jobs (table 3.5), hold wages down, and take more from the economy than they contribute (Davila and Rodriguez 2000; Klineberg 1996). The following comments capture the feelings of African Americans who hold these views.

> They come over across the border and take the most menial jobs, whereas Blacks are not going to take a little of nothing. We want better jobs, but they take the little jobs away from Black Americans and that is the problem. White Anglos give them jobs 'cause they are going to work for $4.25 an hour. As a Black American, I am not going to take $4.25. If I think I'm worth $6.00 an hour, who do you think they are going to hire, me or him? I mean, I got to survive and their survival ways are different than mine. My standards are much higher than theirs. They will take a shack and live with ten or twenty people, whereas I'm going to take my family and try to survive 'cause over the years people have taken things away from Black men and Black Americans.
>
> FORTY-TWO-YEAR-OLD AFRICAN AMERICAN FEMALE
>
> I'm not from Houston, but when I moved here, I saw how these Mexicans run down these jobs. They come in and do jobs for the minimum amount of money and in turn it runs down the pay scale. I really don't see the economic situation getting any

better. Jobs are hard to find, and all these Mexicans work for anything. These perceptions could be improved if they just learn to be more like Blacks and Whites and not work for any amount of money. They can keep the salaries up by not settling for just anything. That's the only way I can see things improve because they really hurt us economically.

TWENTY-EIGHT-YEAR-OLD AFRICAN AMERICAN MALE

However, not all African Americans feel that immigration has a negative impact. For example:

I believe that people aren't going to the root of it. They think that Mexicans come here to take all our jobs, but the thing is, they are in the same situation as a lot of Black people as far as economics and poverty are concerned. They are just trying to solve their problems. They are not necessarily saying, We don't like Black people; let's take their jobs. They're just trying to survive. As a Black person, I believe that tolerance and seeking understanding between the two groups will improve the conditions. We're all in the same boat, so we might as well find out what brings us together and what we have in common instead of concentrating on what divides us and what we don't have in common.

EIGHTEEN-YEAR-OLD AFRICAN AMERICAN MALE

U.S.- and foreign-born Hispanics in Houston see the issue of immigration differently. They do not feel that immigrants take jobs from African Americans (table 3.5), and they perceive the overall effect of immigration as good. As might be expected, Hispanic immigrants share this view in relatively larger numbers than U.S.-born Hispanics.

Are anti-immigrant sentiments grounded in fact? Research on the economic impact of immigration reveals a mixed picture. Some research has found that immigrants replace native-born workers with low levels of education (Camaroto 1997, 1998). There is also some research (DeFreitas 1988) that shows immigrants take jobs from other minorities in local economies that are stagnant and in the secondary labor market where wages are low, benefits nonexistent, and job advancement nil. Given that this is the sector of the economy where many African American women work, their anti-immigrant sentiment becomes understandable. This issue is elaborated in chapter 4.

Other research shows that immigrants do not compete with American-born minorities and that the long-term, overall effect of immigration is positive (Fox and Parsel 1994). Any job displacement that occurs among African Americans is also said to be a function of long-standing discriminatory hiring practices (Camaroto 1997; Fox and Parsel 1994).

The Spanish Language

The use of Spanish by immigrants may contribute to anti-immigrant sentiment among African Americans. The continuous influx of immigrants from Mexico and other Spanish-speaking countries means that the use of the Spanish language in Houston and other parts of the United States has increased. It has led to controversy in the workplace, at schools, and elsewhere in the public sphere (Carrasco 1998; Ferris 1994; Mitchell 1993; Tobar 1992). The most prominent example of negative reaction against the speaking of Spanish is the English Only movement, whose goal is to pass legislation or amend the United States Constitution to make English the official language of the nation.

The controversy over the Spanish language is reflected by African Americans in our survey. Almost as many African Americans indicated that it is okay to speak Spanish in the workplace as stated that Spanish should not be spoken (table 3.5). A similar pattern emerges when African Americans describe the impact of Spanish in the United States. Almost as many individuals say that the impact is good as say that it is negative. The issue was further highlighted in the Black-Brown survey when many African Americans stated that the major difference between the African American and Hispanic communities is language. African Americans who express negative views about the Spanish language tend to be older, thereby suggesting a generational difference. Consider the following comment from a forty-three-year-old Black woman who works with Hispanics:

> Language is the biggest problem here at the store because Blacks only speak English and Hispanics speak both English and Spanish. When Hispanics speak their native language and Blacks can't understand, the first thing that comes out of a Black person's mind is that they are talking about them and this is where the conflict comes in. It's happening everywhere. You have one Black standing in a crowd of Hispanics and they feel that Hispanics should speak English, if they can speak English, but instead they

start speaking Spanish. The first thing that comes out of your mind is, they are talking about me. Blacks don't have the opportunity to speak two languages, they speak only one and that's Afro-American. Blacks feel that if you come to my country you should speak my language. Hispanics feel if you want to know what I'm talking about you should learn my language. That's where the conflict comes in.

Hispanics admit that at times they revert to Spanish and make comments about coworkers. For the most part, however, they are simply carrying on conversations about work-related matters and about normal day-to-day things in a language that they feel more comfortable speaking (Mindiola 1982) or that is the only language they know.

Language has the potential to be a divisive issue. A group's language is an intimate matter. It not only represents the core but also the essence of a culture. To ridicule a group because of its language or to prevent a group from speaking its language is tantamount to saying that its culture and the group itself are inferior. Hispanics have had to deal with these issues throughout much of their history in the United States, but within the past thirty years the bilingual, bicultural movement has emboldened the community and pride in language and culture is at an all-time high. Also, the growing economic and political importance of the Hispanic community has caused many businesses to recruit bilingual employees and many candidates for public office to learn Spanish. Thus if African Americans are seen as partners or strong supporters of efforts to limit the Spanish language, it could have negative repercussions for relations between the groups. On the other hand, if African Americans are seen as supporters of the Spanish language, it could enhance and improve their relations with Hispanics.

Foreign-born Hispanics versus African Americans and U.S.-born Hispanics

Abortion

Abortion is an issue that can be cast along the conservative-liberal continuum, with conservatives strongly opposing legal abortion and liberals supporting the right of women to make a choice. Foreign-born Hispanics tend to be conservative, with a majority opposing legal abortion (see table 3.5). Catholicism and family values that include a central role for children offer possible explanations for this stance. The following comments reveal the anti-abortion sentiment among foreign-born Hispanics.

> I'm Catholic and I'm against abortion. We all have a right to live.
>
> FORTY-EIGHT-YEAR-OLD HISPANIC IMMIGRANT FEMALE

> Abortion should not be legal anywhere, period. I believe that it is a life that is being violated and everyone has a right to live. I don't think that human life should ever be taken, so it [abortion] should not be legal anywhere.
>
> THIRTY-SEVEN-YEAR-OLD HISPANIC IMMIGRANT MALE

In contrast, a majority of African Americans in the survey support legal abortion in the United States. The following brief comment reflects the sentiments of African Americans and suggests why abortion is supported.

> Yes, abortion should remain legal. In certain situations like rape, abortion is definitely an option.
>
> TWENTY-EIGHT-YEAR-OLD AFRICAN AMERICAN FEMALE

The relatively higher rates of abortion and out-of-wedlock births among African Americans may explain their support. In 1998 in Harris County, one out of every three pregnancies among African Americans was aborted, compared to one out of every five for Hispanics. These figures include both U.S.- and foreign-born Hispanics. Sixty-two percent of all African American births in 1998 were out of wedlock, compared to 40 percent for U.S.-born Hispanics and 31 percent for foreign-born Hispanics. The abortion rates are higher in Harris County than for the state as a whole, but the pattern is the same. The out-of-wedlock birth statistics for Harris County are comparable to those of the state of Texas (Texas Bureau of Vital Statistics 1998).

U.S.-born Hispanics, like the U.S. population at large, are split on abortion, with almost equal proportions supporting and not supporting its legality (table 3.5). The different attitudes to abortion between U.S.- and foreign-born Hispanics may reflect different socialization experiences. Mexico, for example, where most of the immigrants are from, is one of the largest Catholic countries in the world, and the Catholic Church is staunchly against abortion. Also, in Mexico abortion is illegal. In the United States, the Catholic Church has more competition from other denominations, some of which support the right of a woman to choose.

Children

The role that children play in the families of foreign-born Hispanics is different from that of African Americans and U.S.-born Hispanics. In Hispanic immigrant families, children who work are expected to make an economic contribution to the household. Approximately 58 percent of Hispanic immigrants in the Black-Brown survey believe that children who work should turn their money over to their parents. Consider the following comments:

> I think children should definitely help their parents because our parents worked for us and now we should help them.
>
> Twenty-one-year-old Hispanic immigrant male

> They [children] have an obligation to give to their parents if they are of working age and they should feel obligated to help their parents.
>
> Forty-eight-year-old Hispanic immigrant female

In contrast, only 33 percent of U.S.-born Hispanics and 26 percent of African Americans feel that working children should turn their money over to their parents (see table 3.5). For example:

> No, I don't think they should because it is unfair to the child who has earned the money. It can be discouraging.
>
> Twenty-eight-year-old African American female

> I don't think it's fair to the child who's working because it's their money; they earned it, not the parents. When I turned eighteen and started working I had to give a large portion of my money to my mother and I didn't like it. I put up a fight because I didn't think it was fair, but I had to anyway.
>
> Twenty-four-year-old U.S.-born Hispanic female

How can these different views be explained? The opinions held by the immigrants may be reflecting the economic basis for group values. Poor economic circumstances promotes the sharing of economic resources and the development of values that enhance the importance of family cooperation. Because Hispanic immigrants come from countries where the

Table 3.6 Responses by Ethnic Groups to Questions about Discrimination and Opportunities

| | % WHO STATE MORE | | |
	U.S.-BORN HISPANICS	FOREIGN-BORN HISPANICS	AFRICAN AMERICANS
Hispanics experience the same, more, or less discrimination than African Americans.	22	51	8
African Americans have the same, more, or fewer opportunities than Hispanics.	37	56	20

economic conditions are far worse than in the United States, everyone in the family who works is expected to cooperate and make a contribution to the sustenance of the family. Many immigrants in Houston send significant portions of their incomes to their homelands to help support their families. Indeed, helping the family back home is the primary reason many immigrants cross the border into the United States.

In contrast, Hispanics who were born and raised in the United States and African Americans reflect another set of economic circumstances. Every working member of the family is not necessarily expected to make a contribution to its collective well-being. Children remain economically dependent on the family for longer periods. If and when they begin to work, they feel that the money they earn is theirs. The United States is a rich country. Mexico and Central America, from which most immigrants originate, are poor regions, where group values take precedence over individualistic values. The exceptions in the United States are found in the lower classes, among whom, in contrast to the middle and upper classes, resources tend to be shared.

Conflict and Race Relations

Most immigrants believe that there is a great deal of conflict between Hispanics and African Americans in Houston (see table 3.5). Many also feel that Hispanics experience more discrimination and have less opportunity and that African Americans are prejudiced against Hispanics (table 3.6).

A significant number of immigrants also express a fear of African

Americans and believe that African Americans have too much power (table 3.5). These views again reveal the social distance and also the degree of mistrust that foreign-born Hispanics have of African Americans. The following remarks reflect a negative evaluation of African American work habits as well as a comment on intergroup relations.

> There is conflict because African Americans believe that they are the only ones who experience discrimination. They don't realize that we too face discrimination. Also, African Americans are lazy and don't like to work, especially if their boss is a Mexicano. This creates conflict.
>
> FIFTY-ONE-YEAR-OLD HISPANIC IMMIGRANT MALE

Another comment reflects awareness of each group's territory and the danger that one can experience when crossing over:

> Yes, I think there is a lot of conflict between us territorial-wise. I mean, for example, in neighborhoods, whether a Black neighborhood or a Mexican neighborhood, you are looked at as a stranger who has nothing to do in that neighborhood. I know when we go to a Black neighborhood we are looked at strange, as if we are looking for trouble. They see us as a threat. You hear of shootings going on between Blacks and Mexicans in neighborhoods. It is a territorial dispute. They see us as if we don't belong here. The same happens with Mexicans when we see Blacks coming into our neighborhoods.
>
> THIRTY-YEAR-OLD HISPANIC IMMIGRANT MALE

Among African Americans there is disagreement about the extent of conflict between the two groups. Almost as many say there is conflict as say there is none. African Americans who see conflict cite competition for jobs, race, political power, and respect as the reasons.

> Hispanics and Blacks compete for jobs, managerial jobs, labor jobs, and hourly jobs. What put this store on the map was the Hispanic people and now they get the opportunity to move up quicker than the other minorities.
>
> THIRTY-THREE-YEAR-OLD AFRICAN AMERICAN FEMALE

> Yes, there is quite a bit of competition and conflict because they are both minorities trying to find a niche in this "White man's"

society. I don't think they realize that if they work together they can get both of their goals accomplished.

Forty-nine-year-old African American male

I think they compete over the racial thing because Hispanics think they are better than the African Americans and they look down on African Americans.

Forty-year-old African American female

In one of the mayoral elections, Mayor Lanier as a candidate got more support from the Hispanic community than from the African American community. And now he is paying back those favors with placements at Metro and using Metro funds to award contracts to Hispanics. There's a great deal of competition between Blacks and Hispanics here right now.

Forty-seven-year-old African American male

African Americans who perceive conflict tend to have less contact with Hispanics. They also believe that as a group African Americans are less united than Hispanics, have less opportunity, and experience more discrimination and that Hispanics have not fought for their rights in the way African Americans have.

It's hard to get African Americans to unify. We've had this problem since slavery. Hispanics are basically a close-knit group and they tend to stick together. If they have an issue they call people to come to a meeting and they show up. If we have an issue and call a meeting we might have ten people show up. I think it's because of their culture. I think Hispanics have such a close family with their parents in control. If the father says, "We're going to a meeting," the whole family will go to the meeting. We have been split up for so long and most of our families are one-parent families and this goes way back in history. But if you deal with a Hispanic, it's the family. They might not get along, and the father might be abusing them, but they stick together.

Fifty-year-old African American male

African Americans experience more discrimination and I believe Hispanics have more opportunity. Why? I think it's because of color. I keep going back to the color thing. I think that has a lot to do with it. Hispanics can assimilate more than a Black person because there is no way a Black person can hide his or her color.

THIRTY-FOUR-YEAR-OLD AFRICAN AMERICAN FEMALE

I think we've been more militant. I think some of the advantages that we have came as a result of the Black outcry and won by the blood and sweat of a lot of Black people. I'm not saying that Hispanics don't work for the good of all, but to be perfectly honest, a lot of the concessions that minorities have today were brought to the forefront by Black leaders. I mean, to be perfectly honest, the Civil Rights Act of 1964, the Desegregation Act, these were brought about because we were on the outside. I think White institutions have always been open to Hispanics.

FORTY-TWO-YEAR-OLD AFRICAN AMERICAN FEMALE

African Americans do not feel that Hispanics fear them or that African Americans have too much power (table 3.5). Fear and power are important components of race relations. Fear can range from one group being physically afraid of another group to fear of one's offspring marrying someone of a different race. Power refers to the relative ability of a group to accomplish its goals in the face of obstacles. Power enters into the dialogue between minorities because it is one of the criteria by which they measure each other's progress and standing in society.

No, I don't think they [Hispanics] fear us. Why should they? What can we do to them? And I don't know what power we have, but we certainly don't have that much power in the political process, especially as it relates to Congress. I don't think either group has that much power.

FIFTY-SEVEN-YEAR-OLD AFRICAN AMERICAN MALE

Power? What power? We have to struggle for everything, and we still don't have equal footing with everyone else, especially the Whites. I don't know how anyone can say we have too much power, unless they don't want us to have anything.

FORTY-THREE-YEAR-OLD AFRICAN AMERICAN FEMALE

Approximately 42 percent of African Americans and 41 percent of U.S.-born Hispanics did not see much conflict between Hispanics and African Americans.

If there is conflict I have never seen it or read about it in the papers or experienced it myself. They, Hispanics and Blacks, are at the same level, and the only thing both groups are trying to do, is to at least get to where the White race is. So no, I don't think there is competition. Both groups are just trying to get some recognition.

Thirty-nine-year-old African American male

In my dealings with Hispanics, I haven't seen conflict. The work environment that I have been in, and the one I'm in now, I don't see conflict between Blacks and Hispanics for the simple reason that everybody is out to get a piece of the pie, everybody is out to do their best. And as far as you know, this Black is this and this Hispanic is that, I don't see it.

Fifty-one-year-old African American male

Well, politically, if they are running for the office, yes, there's competition, but overall, I don't feel that conflict is a major problem or a big issue between the groups.

Fifty-five-year-old U.S.-born Hispanic female

No, I don't think there's conflict. Here at work, we work together, do things together and get along.

Thirty-seven-year-old U.S.-born Hispanic male

Who Do Anglos Favor or Fear the Most?

Central to relations between Hispanics and African Americans is the relationship that each group has with the Anglo population. Although Hispanics and African Americans have made gains in recent years, especially in the political arena, Anglos still control the economic resources and thus have tremendous influence on the minority communities. African Americans and U.S.-born Hispanics reveal a split between those who feel that Anglos do not have a preference and those who feel that Anglos prefer Hispanics.

I don't feel that Anglos favor anyone but themselves. What they do is play the minorities against each other and they do whatever it takes for them to hold on to their position. If that takes catering to African Americans on an issue they will do it, if it takes catering to Hispanics on an issue they will do it. Personally, I don't think they favor one or the other.

THIRTY-FIVE-YEAR-OLD AFRICAN AMERICAN MALE

They favor us [Hispanics] because we're so docile. With Blacks, you push them and they'll push back. With us, they give us a little bit of money, a little bit of a title, a little bit of a position, and we are not going to make any demands. They have more respect for the Black community because they know that they can push them only so far and Blacks will start pushing back.

FORTY-SIX-YEAR-OLD U.S.-BORN HISPANIC FEMALE

Foreign-born Hispanics feel that Anglos prefer African Americans.

They favor the African American. They listen to the African American because African Americans are united. Hispanics are not united, and instead of helping each other, we work against each other.

THIRTY-THREE-YEAR-OLD HISPANIC IMMIGRANT FEMALE

I think Anglos prefer African Americans because they understand each other and have the same culture. The Anglo understands the African American much more than the Hispanic.

TWENTY-ONE-YEAR-OLD HISPANIC IMMIGRANT MALE

In regard to who Anglos fear, the responses of each subsample split between those who feel that Anglos fear Hispanics and African Americans to the same degree and those who feel that Anglos fear African Americans more than they fear Hispanics.

I don't know if fear is the right word, but I don't think that Anglos are scared of one group more than the other. I think they are wary of both groups because both are pushing for things that threaten them. Both groups want more recognition, more political positions, better jobs. Anglos fear African Americans because African Americans fight for their rights.

TWENTY-ONE-YEAR-OLD HISPANIC MALE IMMIGRANT

I think they fear us more, definitely, because of our history, our struggles, our color, and White guilt over the way we have been treated. They fear our ability to make change. We have challenged the laws, the economic structure, the social norms, everything. Other minorities may be coming up but they pattern their efforts after ours because we have had a degree of success.

FIFTY-ONE-YEAR-OLD AFRICAN AMERICAN FEMALE

The empirical information suggests that Anglos favor Hispanics and fear African Americans. Intermarriage and residential integration rates show that Anglos and Hispanics intermarry more (Valdez 1999) and live in closer proximity to each other than do Anglos and African Americans (*Houston Chronicle,* April 15, 2001). This means that there is much more interaction between Anglos and Hispanics and greater acceptance of Hispanics that is not found between Anglos and African Americans. Thus it appears that Anglos would be more amenable to forming coalitions with Hispanics and more likely to keep a large segment of the Hispanic population from forming alliances with African Americans.

The Effects of Social Class

Social class position seems to be more important in explaining the views of African Americans than in shedding light on the views of U.S.- and foreign-born Hispanics. Using educational attainment and level of income as indicators of social class, the Black-Brown survey indicates that African Americans in the middle and higher classes (high levels of education attainment and higher incomes) disagree more than lower-class African Americans that their group is prejudiced against Hispanics. Middle- and higher-status African Americans also disagree that African Americans have too much power and that African Americans fear Hispanics. They also see immigration in a more positive light. They do not think that immigrants take jobs from African Americans, and they believe that the overall effect of immigration is positive. That middle- and upper-class African Americans report more interaction with Hispanics may explain their more positive views. Lower-status African Americans may feel more threatened by immigrants because of their perception that immigrants compete with them for jobs. To the extent that immigrants do indeed affect the occupational status of African Americans it tends to occur in the low-paying occupations where immigrants compete with African Americans. The converse may also be true; that is, higher-status African Americans have less resentful attitudes toward immigrants because they do not compete with them in the job market.

Among U.S.-born Hispanics, the educational and income indicators of social class do not explain differences in their opinions about African Americans. The only exceptions deal with fear and interaction. U.S.-born Hispanics with higher levels of education and income do not feel that Hispanics fear African Americans while lower-class U.S.-born Hispanics do believe that Hispanics fear African Americans. Also, those in the middle and upper classes report more interaction with African Americans than do the lower classes. Again, frequent interaction with African Americans may explain the more positive opinions of the higher classes.

Education and income levels do not distinguish the opinions of Hispanic immigrants. Of course, it could be that most of the foreign born tend to have the same opinions regardless of class positions. Only future research can resolve these questions.

Conclusion

African Americans and Hispanics disagree on the effects of immigration and the speaking of Spanish in the workplace and in their perceptions of conflict. It is important to note, however, that not only do African Americans disagree with Hispanics on these issues, African Americans themselves are divided in their opinions. Recall that African American respondents were almost evenly divided between those who perceived the effect of immigration as positive and those who viewed it as negative. They were also evenly divided on the speaking of Spanish. Thus a coalition, say, in support of immigration could potentially exist between U.S.- and foreign-born Hispanics and perhaps as much as half of the adult African American community.

On the other hand, the potential for such a coalition could dissipate if immigration increases and is accompanied by an increase in the number of African Americans who perceive immigrants as a threat. Recently there was talk that an amnesty program for undocumented Mexican residents in the United States would be proposed by the presidents of the United States and Mexico. The proposal reportedly will include a guest worker program that will allow Mexicans to work in the United States and an increase in the number of Mexicans who are permitted to migrate to the United States legally. The guest worker program could pose a threat to lower-class African Americans, and increasing the number of legal migrants may result in more middle-class Mexicans migrating and competing with middle-class Blacks. Also, making undocumented Mexican immigrants "legal" will probably stimulate more undocumented migration to the United States because it will signal the continued availability of jobs and a more welcoming attitude. It is probably the case that just talking about these issues in public stimulates migration. More migration could instigate more cultural tension over the use of Spanish and the perception that Hispanics are becoming a dominant group because of high rates of growth and government favoritism.

An issue that clearly divides Hispanics and African Americans is the perception among Hispanics that government programs designed to help minorities favor African Americans. More foreign-born Hispanics express this opinion than Hispanics born in the United States. Hispanics may feel this way because it was African Americans who initiated and led the civil rights movement. Also, foreign-born Hispanics are ineligible to receive many government services because they are not citizens. Federal scholarships, for example, are available only to U.S. citizens.

African Americans disagree that government programs favor them. This difference in perception could lead Hispanics to withdraw their support of such programs, but thus far this has not occurred. A recent referendum on whether Houston's affirmative action programs should continue received broad support from both African Americans and Hispanics and could not have passed without the support of both groups, especially the extraordinary turnout of African American voters. Further and more important, the perception among Hispanics that African Americans benefit more from affirmative action is incorrect. Research shows that more Hispanics than African Americans have benefited from Houston's affirmative action programs in terms of the total number of contracts awarded and total dollar amounts (Santos 1999). Widespread knowledge of this would not necessarily create harmony between the groups since it could be seen as unfair and occurring at the expense of African Americans. The solution, of course, is that both groups benefit in an equitable manner, but as long as they do not, affirmative action programs will continue to be a contentious issue and could lead to one group withdrawing its support. At the moment, in Houston this does not seem likely, nor does it seem that affirmative action programs face the threat of being eliminated through the referendum process. It nevertheless has the potential to be an issue, especially among middle- and upper-middle-class Hispanic and African Americans who tend to be the beneficiaries of affirmative action programs.

The second pattern that emerged from the survey is how the views of foreign-born Hispanics differ on some issues not only from the views of African Americans but also from the opinions of U.S.-born Hispanics. The greater antipathy between foreign-born Hispanics and African Americans has already been mentioned in previous chapters. Foreign-born Hispanics have more negative views of African Americans and there is a greater social distance between them and African Americans. It is not surprising, therefore, that foreign-born Hispanics and African Americans also hold different views on abortion, children, and issues related to race relations, such as who experiences the most discrimination, has the most opportunity, relations with Anglos, and whether African Americans are prejudiced against Hispanics. The important question here is, given how little contact Hispanic immigrants have with African Americans, what is the cause of their negative perceptions? One explanation is that there are universal negative perceptions of Black people perpetuated by the media, which now have a global reach. Thus a person from Mexico migrating to Houston or elsewhere in the United States comes with perceptions that may be reinforced once here. The following statement by a college student born in Mexico speaks to this issue but not only in regard to African Americans.

I did not have any contact with African Americans before I came to the United States because there are very few if any in Mexico. Everything I knew or thought about Blacks came from television in Mexico and the movies and most of what I thought was negative. Here in the United States I learned to fear them because of everything you hear and see. Only recently have I started to see things differently, but most definitely I had an image of them when I came from Mexico and it came from the media, but I can also say the same thing about Anglos. I did not know any Anglos in Mexico and my opinions of them also came from television, but they were not as negative.

TWENTY-FOUR-YEAR-OLD HISPANIC FEMALE

Thus the lack of interaction with African Americans does not necessarily mean that foreign-born Hispanics do not already have negative perceptions of African Americans. More likely, little or no interaction means that many Hispanic immigrants are not afforded the opportunity to change their opinions.

Also, recall that the opinions of the foreign born differ from the U.S. born on these issues as well. In other words, the views of U.S.-born Hispanics are more like the views of African Americans and less like the views of foreign-born Hispanics, at least on these issues. A relevant research question here is whether the cultural and racial affinity between immigrants and U.S.-born Hispanics make their differences of opinion more amenable to reconciliation in comparison to the differences of opinion between immigrants and African Americans.

On some issues, the foreign born themselves are divided. One example is whether Hispanics fear African Americans. The foreign born are almost evenly split in their opinions. On other issues, such as prejudice against Hispanics, about one-third of the foreign born do not believe that African Americans are prejudiced against them. This tells us that on some issues there are differences of opinion between Hispanics and African Americans, regardless of whether Hispanics are born here or elsewhere. On other issues, most U.S.-born Hispanics and African Americans hold views that are similar to each other and that are at odds with the opinions of foreign-born Hispanics. Still, on other issues, African Americans, U.S.- born Hispanics, and foreign-born Hispanics may themselves be divided on an issue.

The implications of these issues for conflict or coalition between African Americans and Hispanics are discussed in more detail in chapter 6.

Chapter 4

Women's Perceptions of Black-Brown Relations: A Contextual Approach

I get along with women of color; we may not be of the same culture, but we relate because we know how it feels to be the minority, both as women and as people of color.

AFRICAN AMERICAN FEMALE

Blacks pretend they don't see the Hispanic women waiting for services; they "talk down" to us, and treat us very disrespectfully, and claim they don't understand us, even when we speak English.

HISPANIC FEMALE

Black and Hispanic women hold more hostile attitudes toward each other's groups than do their male counterparts. This finding in our preliminary analyses took us by surprise. We had set out to examine relations between the two largest ethnic-racial minority groups in the United States, not expecting that our findings would be gender-driven. We conducted confirmatory analyses and speculated about how to best understand this conclusion. Here we discuss our findings from data-driven and conceptual, analytic approaches. We employ a feminist perspective to speculate about the foundations of women's relatively more negative attitudes, compared to men.[1]

It is fair to say we were surprised by our findings because the role of women in shaping intergroup attitudes and group relations has been largely ignored. The social science research, on which we were relying, has generally reflected the assumptions of the current patriarchal system in the United States in seeing men as the institutional leaders in their respective communities and families. In this chapter we begin to address this major oversight by taking a contextual approach to understanding women's roles in intergroup relations. Foremost in this approach is an understanding that African American and Hispanic women are a triple minority: they experience the consequences of their gender in a patriarchal society, they hold a low socioeconomic status in a capitalistic system, and they are racial minorities who lack power in the United States. As a result, African American and Hispanic women are subject to sexism, classism, and racism. We begin to explore the implications for intergroup relations by examining women's role in shaping the intergroup attitudes of their children, which in turn affects present and future relations between Hispanics and African Americans.

The Role of Parents in Shaping Children's Racial Attitudes

Adults assume that children learn about racism and race somewhere else, not in the home (Van Ausdale and Feagin 2001, 3). But as early as three years of age children may have constant, well-defined, and negative biases toward racial or ethnic others (Van Ausdale and Feagin 2001). By age seven, when children's cognitive capacities are more fully developed, their ideas and lay theories about other groups remain constant (Cameron et al. 2001). Thus essentialist reasoning is present in young children's conception of race (Hughes 1997). By "essentialist," we refer to thinking about group members in terms of ostensibly inherent and static traits; for example, Latinos are family oriented, Blacks are musical. In other words, by three to seven years old, children expect their racial identities to be linked to family background (e.g., they look like their parents), inherited (e.g., they act like their parents), and impervious to environmental influence (e.g., that's just the way they are).

How is it that children's beliefs about other ethnic-racial groups are formed so early in life? Research in this area concludes that learning prejudices and the subtleties of racially based power relations seems to be, to a great extent, a matter of learning "the ways things are" (Hughes 1997; Trager and Yarrow 1952, 347). At an early age, children adopt adult values and behavior patterns in learning prejudices. Parents are highly influential in socializing their children with respect to this racial-ethnic group knowledge as their "attitudes toward groups enter into the control of their children's social relationships at home, in the neighborhood, and at school" (Trager and Yarrow 1952, 226). As parents socialize their children about other groups, they are teaching their children how to think about Hispanics and African Americans and the relations between the two groups.

Parents' prejudices are expressed through encouragements, admonitions, and restrictions on their children's social lives. Findings indicate that (1) parents' differentiation of groups is reproduced in the children's attempts to differentiate; (2) both parents and children express more hostility toward some groups than toward others; and (3) greater numbers of children than parents express extreme hostility toward one group or another, most likely because of children's frankness and lack of inhibition rather than from greater hostility (Trager and Yarrow 1952).

Parents shape their children's attitudes about other groups by instructing them by example and by rewarding them, consciously or unconsciously, for expressing certain views about out-groups (Worchel 1999). Direct instruction can be positive, negative, or both. Parents can tell a child that a particular group is criminal or that it is polite, respectful, or religious. Parents also instruct children to distinguish between the public and the private sphere. Public norms prohibit negative comments about other groups that can later be contradicted in private and informal settings. Parents can also prohibit or encourage their children to have contact or interaction with different groups. Without the opportunity for positive interaction between Hispanic and African American children, parental responsibility for relations between the groups increases.

Children imitate their parents' intergroup attitudes and behaviors more than is commonly assumed. According to Aboud, "Children learn to evaluate groups the way their parents do either by direct training or by observing and imitating their parents' verbal and nonverbal behavior" (1988, 18). If parents believe that members of other groups are allies, neighbors, coworkers, and, in general, fellow citizens, they will pass on this perception to their children. Consequently, relations between racial-ethnic groups may be enhanced as children become socially and politically aware. On the other hand, if parents believe that members of these groups are prejudiced against them or express prejudice against or fear of a particular group, they pass on those attitudes. As a result, intergroup hostility and conflict increase.

Parents directly or indirectly reward and punish children for compliance or noncompliance with their dictates regarding other groups. Children know their parents' attitudes toward other groups and generally want to please their parents. By behaving in a manner consistent with parents' views about out-groups, including verbal comments, children avoid punishment and may be rewarded. Rewards may be as subtle as sharing a knowing smile after a behavior or verbalization.

Children also learn the subtle dynamics of racially based power relations at a young age (Hughes 1997). This knowledge seems to have a culturally shared dimension that makes prejudice a collective, group-based phenomenon (Bobo 1999). For instance, prejudice may be related to beliefs about a groups' position or status in the social hierarchy. These culturally shared ideas are generally passed on to succeeding generations through socialization (Bobo 1999), which is shaped mostly by parents in interaction with environment.

Of course, children also learn these culturally shared ideas from their peers (Van Ausdale and Feagin 2001). However, these peers often learn their attitudes from their parents, thus ensuring a cycle of negative racial attitudes. Ordinarily children do not try to develop relationships with those in other racial-ethnic groups unless they are directed to do so by teachers or other significant adults (Van Ausdale and Feagin 2001, 28). It is parents or guardians who are likely to be the most significant persons in the lives of children.

The Special Role of Women in Parenting

Women have always been the most important actors in the socialization and nurturing process. Whether by patriarchal design or by choice, it is women who typically play the dominant role in rearing children. Women have closer and more frequent contact with children, and the mother is typically the first parent children imitate. Typically it is women who reward or punish in day-to-day children's activities. Even admonitions such as "Wait until your father gets home" are indirect forms of punishment. In general, women are the primary reproducers of culture through their closer contact and interactions with children. This nurturing and primary child-rearing role of women continues in most households even when women work outside the home. We can expect, then, that although both parents play strong roles in children's lives, women have a primary role in shaping the intergroup attitudes and behaviors of their children.

Women's Role in Children's Socialization about Race

U.S.-born Hispanic Women

Although Hispanic women in the United States have lower status and less power in society in general as well as relative to their male counterparts, they do experience one significant form of power: social influence over children (Vasquez 1984, 1995). In Hispanic culture mothers are highly respected. In traditional, patriarchal Hispanic households the woman's role is that of nurturer and principal caretaker of children (Casas et al. 1995; Davis and Chavez 1995). Although men are increasingly contributing more to what traditionally have been considered women's responsibilities, including child care, the child care role for women is culturally entrenched, even in households where Latinos are house husbands (Davis and Chavez 1995). This nurturing role for Hispanic women dates to pre-Columbian culture (Mirandé and Enríquez 1979). Furthermore, when Hispanic women grow older, their status in the community increases: they are seen as respected *abuelas* (grandmothers) and community elders (Facio 1996). Evidence that Hispanic mothers transmit their values, including those having to do with other groups, to their children is found in the positive correlation between the values of Hispanic mothers and those of their children (Rodriguez, Ramirez, and Korman 1999). The correlation between fathers' and children's values is substantially weaker.

Foreign-born Hispanic Women

Although foreign-born Hispanic women have parenting styles similar to those of the U.S. born, there are important differences in perceptions and attitudes. These differences may be grounded in historical treatment in the United States and in contact with other U.S. ethnic and racial groups. The foreign born tend to be more conservative than the U.S. born, who carry a blend of two cultures—White and Hispanic. The foreign born are closer to their culture of origin and thus retain its values. Because of the relative segregation and isolation of immigrant women in domestic service, agriculture, canneries, sweatshops, and other low-wage employment (Hossfeld 1994; Segura 1994; Zavella 1987), foreign-born Hispanic women have less contact with African Americans than do U.S.-born Hispanic women. This lack of contact with African Americans may mean that it is group stereotypes that are their main source of information about African Americans. The stereotypes often provide distorted and largely negative images of group members (Niemann and Secord 1995; Niemann et al. 1994). The media are an especially powerful source of information for those with little direct contact with African Americans, especially recent immigrants. Social class may be a predictor of some forms of prejudice as members of lower classes are often pitted against each other in competition for resources (Dyer, Vedlitz, and Worchel 1989). Foreign-born Hispanics, with less access to economic opportunities than their U.S.-born counterparts, will be more likely to express prejudicial attitudes. Taken together, these factors increase the likelihood that U.S.-born and foreign-born Hispanics will have significantly different perceptions of African Americans.

African American Women

African American women also have the dominant role in their children's socialization. Like Hispanic mothers, African American mothers are held in high esteem by their children and in their communities.

A survival strategy for Black Americans lies in the transfer of knowledge of women's experiences from one generation to the next (Essed 1990). For instance, African Americans are made aware of racism as children, so they incorporate discussions of racism in the socialization of their own children (Essed 1990). In addition, African American women teach their children to be independent and assertive earlier than do Hispanic women. Assertiveness includes awareness of prejudicial attitudes and appropriate defense strategies against discrimination. In addition, African American women are more individualistic than Hispanic women, who are more group oriented. These cultural differences affect how mothers prepare their children to deal with relations with other groups. African American women's individualism may serve to encourage their children to engage in contact with members of other groups. The quality of this contact will depend in part on the attitudes the children have adopted from their mothers.

Implications of Women's Parenting Role
for Group Relations

It is in their roles as the principal caretakers of children that racial-ethnic women pose the largest political threat to the dominant society. Women and their children are the core around which group solidarity is constructed (Gilkes 1994, 243).

The most important source of discontent for women of color is the effect of racial oppression on the lives of their children and on their day-to-day struggles to provide for their families' needs (Gilkes 1994). Since minority families are not accorded the institutional and ideological supports that benefit White families, women of color find their historical role organized around the nurturance and defense and advancement of an oppressed public family (Gilkes 1994, 242). These social roles as nurturers and defenders of their families and communities and as members of racially oppressed groups keep women from uniting with other oppressed women's racial groups. They also ensure that women pass on their hostile attitudes about other groups to their children, especially when the other groups are seen as contributing to their oppression. Women see their primary responsibility as focusing on the survival of their own families, even to the detriment of all other groups. Anything that is perceived as interfering with or impeding this goal can be the foundation for women's greater intergroup hostility, compared to their male counterparts. Ironically, in the name of providing for their children, by passing on negative beliefs and perceptions, women may be ensuring, consciously or unconsciously, that future relations between Hispanics and African Americans will be negative. In the context of the rapidly changing demographics of the United States, such behavior is destructive to both groups.

What attitudes may our respondents be passing on to the children? Below we compare intergroup perceptions held by men and women of each group and by U.S.-born and foreign-born Hispanics.

Gender, Race, and Country of Origin in Intergroup Relations

Gender

Foreign-born Hispanic females more than foreign-born Hispanic males think that African Americans are prejudiced against Hispanics and have too much power and that both groups fear each other. Also, foreign-born women have less interaction than foreign-born men with African Americans and do not think that the impact of immigration is bad (table 4.1). U.S.-born Hispanic females, more than U.S.-born males, think that African Americans are prejudiced against Hispanics, that Hispanics fear African Americans, and that Anglos favor African Americans (table 4.2). More African American females than males do not believe that African Americans have too much power and that government programs designed to help minorities favor African Americans (table 4.3). African American women are also more likely than African American men to think that immigrants take jobs from African Americans and that the impact of immigration is bad. It is clear that on several of the issues females

Table 4.1 Intergroup Conflict Items with Means for Foreign-born Hispanic Males and Females

ITEM	MALES	FEMALES	F	P-VALUE
There is much conflict between Hispanics and African Americans.[a]	3.27	3.50	2.55	.11
Hispanics are prejudiced against African Americans.[a]	2.41	2.77	5.50	.02*
African Americans are prejudiced against Hispanics.[a]	3.08	3.32	2.14	.14
African Americans have too much power.[a*]	2.49	2.96	9.13	.01**
Hispanics fear African Americans.[a]	2.50	2.85	4.82	.03*
African Americans fear Hispanics.[a]	2.29	1.94	6.63	.01**
Most government programs destined for minorities favor African Americans.[a]	3.38	3.57	1.66	.20
Immigrants take jobs from African Americans.[a]	1.77	1.57	2.35	.13
Anglos favor African Americans.[b]	1.83	1.85	.043	.83
African Americans have more opportunities than Hispanics.[b]	1.51	1.47	.371	.54
Hispanics experience more discrimination than African Americans.[b]	1.61	1.59	.130	.72
How often do you interact with African Americans?[c]	2.06	2.50	13.08	.001***
What is the impact of immigrants in Houston?[d]	1.98	2.23	8.01	.01**
In general, would you say relations between Hispanics and African Americans are . . .[d]	2.14	2.26	2.23	.14

* Statistically significant at $p < .05$; **$p < .01$; ***$p < .001$; ****$p < .0001$
[a] scale: 1 = strongly disagree–5 = strongly agree
[b] scale: 1 = about the same; 2 = more; 3 = less; 4 = refused; 5 = don't know
[c] scale: 1 = frequently; 2 = sometimes; 3 = almost never; 4 = never
[d] scale: 1 = very good; 2 = somewhat good; 3 = somewhat bad; 4 = very bad

Table 4.2 Intergroup Conflict Items with Means for U.S.-born Hispanic Males and Females

Item	Males	Females	F	P-Value
There is much conflict between Hispanics and African Americans.[a]	2.95	3.13	1.09	.30
Hispanics are prejudiced against African Americans.[a]	2.15	2.32	1.01	.32
African Americans are prejudiced against Hispanics.[a]	2.40	2.78	4.22	.04*
African Americans have too much power.[a*]	2.11	2.34	1.61	.20
Hispanics fear African Americans.[a]	1.96	2.43	7.36	.01**
African Americans fear Hispanics.[a]	2.04	1.77	2.32	.07
Most government programs destined for minorities favor African Americans.[a]	3.13	3.18	.056	.89
Immigrants take jobs from African Americans.[a]	2.17	2.08	.187	.67
Anglos favor African Americans.[b]	2.28	2.02	6.69	.01**
African Americans have more opportunities than Hispanics.[b]	1.74	1.69	.367	.55
Hispanics experience more discrimination than African Americans.[b]	2.17	2.07	1.17	.28
How often do you interact with Hispanics?[c]	1.48	1.65	2.06	.15
What is the impact of immigrants in Houston?[d]	2.30	2.48	2.67	.10
In general, would you say relations between Hispanics and African Americans are . . .[d]	2.07	2.02	.440	.51

*Statistically significant at $p < .05$; **$p < .01$; ***$p < .001$; ****$p < .0001$
[a] scale: 1 = strongly disagree–5 = strongly agree
[b] scale: 1 = about the same; 2 = more; 3 = less; 4 = refused; 5 = don't know
[c] scale: 1 = frequently; 2 = sometimes; 3 = almost never; 4 = never
[d] scale: 1 = very good; 2 = somewhat good; 3 = somewhat bad; 4 = very bad

Table 4.3 Intergroup Conflict Items with Means
for African American Males and Females

ITEM	MALES	FEMALES	F	P-VALUE
There is much conflict between Hispanics and African Americans.[a]	3.02	3.01	.018	.89
Hispanics are prejudiced against African Americans.[a]	2.78	2.70	.432	.51
African Americans are prejudiced against Hispanics.[a]	2.14	2.09	.247	.61
African Americans have too much power.[a]*	1.64	1.85	4.30	.04*
Hispanics fear African Americans.[a]	2.22	2.02	3.33	.07
African Americans fear Hispanics.[a]	1.52	1.47	.392	.53
Most government programs destined for minorities favor African Americans.[a]	1.99	1.77	4.82	.03*
Immigrants take jobs from African Americans.[a]	3.14	3.51	6.76	.01**
Anglos favor African Americans.[b]	1.64	1.74	2.88	.09
African Americans have more opportunities than Hispanics.[b]	1.90	1.86	.329	.57
Hispanics experience more discrimination than African Americans.[b]	1.55	1.60	.929	.33
How often do you interact with Hispanics?[c]	1.29	1.47	10.20	.001***
What is the impact of immigrants in Houston?[d]	2.61	2.95	18.89	.0001****
In general, would you say relations between Hispanics and African Americans are . . .[d]	2.32	2.40	.795	.37

* Statistically significant at $p < .05$; ** $p < .01$; *** $p < .001$; **** $p < .0001$
[a] scale: 1 = strongly disagree–5 = strongly agree
[b] scale: 1 = about the same; 2 = more; 3 = less; 4 = refused; 5 = don't know
[c] scale: 1 = frequently; 2 = sometimes; 3 = almost never; 4 = never
[d] scale: 1 = very good; 2 = somewhat good; 3 = somewhat bad; 4 = very bad

in each of the subsamples view the relationship between Hispanics and African Americans much more negatively than do males.

Race

Hispanic women generally see the relationship between themselves and African Americans more negatively than do African American women, as indicated in table 4.4. Hispanic women believe the following: African Americans are prejudiced against them, African Americans have too much power, Hispanics fear African Americans, African Americans fear Hispanics, government programs favor African Americans, Anglos favor African Americans, Hispanics experience more discrimination, and Hispanics do not interact with African Americans. African American women, compared to Hispanic women, are more likely to believe that relations with Hispanics are poor, to see the impact of immigrants as bad, and to agree that immigrants take jobs from African Americans.

Country of Origin

Among Hispanic women the foreign born define the relationship with African Americans more negatively than do the U.S. born. This is illustrated on thirteen of the fourteen items shown in table 4.4. To summarize, foreign-born Hispanic women see more conflict between the two groups, think both groups are prejudiced against each other, believe that government programs favor African Americans, do not think immigrants take jobs from African Americans, feel that African Americans have more opportunity and that Hispanics experience more discrimination, interact less with African Americans, and think that the impact of immigration is good and that the relationship between the groups is bad.

Women's Intergroup Attitudes in Their Own Voices

Blacks pretend they don't see the Hispanic women waiting for services; they "talk down" to us, and treat us very disrespectfully, and claim they don't understand us, even when we speak English.

Hispanic female

We conducted focus groups to clarify survey findings. The participants in the Hispanic focus groups were recent arrivals, women who were born in the United States, college students, and young adults not in school. The educational levels of the women ranged from no formal education

Table 4.4 Intergroup Conflict Items with Means for U.S.- and Foreign-born Hispanic Females and African American Females

ITEM	U.S.-BORN FEMALES	FOREIGN-BORN FEMALES	AFRICAN AMERICAN FEMALES
There is much conflict between Hispanics and African Americans.[a]	3.13	3.50	3.01
Hispanics are prejudiced against African Americans.[a]	2.32	2.77	2.70
African Americans are prejudiced against Hispanics.[a]	2.78	3.32	2.09
African Americans have too much power.[a]	2.34	2.99	1.85
Hispanics fear African Americans.[a]	2.43	2.85	2.02
African Americans fear Hispanics.[a]	1.77	1.94	1.47
Most government programs destined for minorities favor African Americans.[a]	3.18	3.57	1.77
Immigrants take jobs from African Americans.[a]	2.08	1.57	3.51
Anglos favor African Americans.[b]	2.02	1.85	1.74
African Americans have more opportunities than Hispanics.[b]	1.69	1.47	1.86
Hispanics experience more discrimination than African Americans.[b]	2.07	1.59	1.60
How often do you interact with Hispanics?[c]	1.65	2.50	1.47
What is the impact of immigrants in Houston?[d]	2.48	2.23	2.95
In general, would you say relations between Hispanics and African Americans are . . .[d]	2.02	2.26	2.40

[a] scale: 1 = strongly disagree–5 = strongly agree
[b] scale: 1 = about the same; 2 = more; 3 = less; 4 = refused; 5 = don't know
[c] scale: 1 = frequently; 2 = sometimes; 3 = almost never; 4 = never
[d] scale: 1 = very good; 2 = somewhat good; 3 = somewhat bad; 4 = very bad

Table 4.5 Intergroup Conflict Items with Means for U.S.- and Foreign-born Hispanic Females

Item	U.S.-born Females	Foreign-born Females	F	P-Value
There is much conflict between Hispanics and African Americans.[a]	3.13	3.50	4.69	.01**
Hispanics are prejudiced against African Americans.[a]	2.32	2.77	4.99	.01**
African Americans are prejudiced against Hispanics.[a]	2.78	3.32	7.04	.0001***
African Americans have too much power.[a]*	2.34	2.99	8.83	.0001***
Hispanics fear African Americans.[a]	2.43	2.85	3.98	.05*
African Americans fear Hispanics.[a]	1.77	1.94	1.27	.28
Most government programs destined for minorities favor African Americans.[a]	3.18	3.57	3.59	.05*
Immigrants take jobs from African Americans.[a]	2.08	1.57	7.03	.0001***
Anglos favor African Americans.[b]	2.02	1.85	2.88	.06
African Americans have more opportunities than Hispanics.[b]	1.69	1.47	6.10	.01**
Hispanics experience more discrimination than African Americans.[b]	2.07	1.59	18.58	.0001****
How often do you interact with African Americans?[c]	1.65	2.50	25.85	.0001****
What is the impact of immigrants in Houston?[d]	2.48	2.23	3.92	.02*
In general, would you say relations between Hispanics and African Americans are . . .[d]	2.02	2.26	8.44	.001***

* Statistically significant at $p < .05$; ** $p < .01$; *** $p < .001$; **** $p < .0001$
[a] scale: 1 = strongly disagree–5 = strongly agree
[b] scale: 1 = about the same; 2 = more; 3 = less; 4 = refused; 5 = don't know
[c] scale: 1 = frequently; 2 = sometimes; 3 = almost never; 4 = never
[d] scale: 1 = very good; 2 = somewhat good; 3 = somewhat bad; 4 = very bad

to currently enrolled in college. The African American women were included only in focus groups with a college student sample. Their voices were further supplemented by individual interviews in their communities. The responses of focus group and interview participants amplified what we found in the survey.

Foreign-born Hispanic women said they encountered a great deal of discrimination by African Americans in places where the following types of public services are dispensed: the Women, Infants, and Children Program [WIC], food stamps, Aid for Families with Dependent Children [AFDC] offices, and health clinics. Most of their contact with African American women occurred at these locales.

In one emotional exchange, a woman told the story of having had her child go hungry at school, even though he had a lunch card. She reported that the Black female workers in the cafeteria and the Black teachers did not ask about his card, they only asked for $1.50, the cost of the lunch. When he told them he did not have $1.50 they replied that he could not eat, even when he said he was hungry. Other women told of similar incidents, and all agreed that "[o]ne of the biggest differences between Hispanic women and Black and Anglo American women is that Hispanic women would never let a child go hungry if they could help it; Hispanic women would find a way to feed the child, even if they had to sacrifice their own lunch to do it." Again, the mostly foreign-born respondents in these focus groups indicated that they had very poor relations with African Americans.

The African American college students stated that Black and Hispanic women sometimes compete for the attention of men. One Black woman said, "I think negatively one of the ways we contribute to intergroup relations is that, when Black women see a brother with a Hispanic girlfriend, we immediately assume that all Mexican women are taking all the brothers away from us, and so you know we have this thing against the Mexican women." This sentiment was supported by another Black woman: "Women become close in work and school situations. I feel that the relationship between these women is positive when there is not a threat of competition." Positive statements among Hispanic and African American college student respondents indicate that in the university setting, both groups are minorities as women and people of color and need to stick together.

Discussion of Results

Hispanic and African American women have more negative attitudes and perceptions about each other's group than do their male counterparts. Among Hispanic women, the U.S.-born perceive better relations with African Americans than do the foreign-born. These perceptions can be divided into two main types—those related to prejudice and those related to political power. Given women's dominant role in nurturing and socializing children and the increasing number of Hispanic immigrants in the United States, there are important implications of these findings for future intergroup relations.

For example, Hispanic women believe that Hispanics fear African Americans. This fear may be grounded in Hispanics' stereotypes of African Americans as criminally inclined (Niemann et al. 1994). The Hispanic foreign born, in particular, may rely on stereotypic information more than the U.S.-born because they have less contact with African Americans. Hispanic women's fear of Blacks may also be grounded in their intimidation by Black women in places that provide services for low-income people. It seems likely that Hispanic men's experiences with Black males differ importantly from Hispanic women's experiences with Black females. Nevertheless, Hispanic women's fear of African Americans has implications for social distance between the groups. As women pass on this fear to their children, they could contribute to lessened contact, increased hostility, and generally negative relations between the groups.

Hispanic women's fear of African Americans seems inseparable from their prejudice against them. Among Hispanics, women believe more than men that Hispanics are prejudiced against Blacks. This belief is likely a reflection of the respondents' own prejudicial attitudes, indicating that among Hispanics, women may be more prejudiced than men. These attitudes could also increase the social distance between these groups in the future as the beliefs of the mothers are passed on to their children (Aboud 1988). As Hispanic children are taught prejudice against and fear of African Americans, the prospects of future cooperation between the groups decrease. African American women, more than men, also believe that Hispanics are prejudiced against their group.

Although African American women do not fear Hispanics physically, they do see Hispanics as competition for resources. This finding is not surprising given that Black women, more than Black men, have the role of protecting their children and providing for the needs of their families.

African American women see Hispanics as taking resources they need for their own families and for themselves. Therefore, as Black women interact with Hispanics more than their male counterparts, this sense of competition likely has an impact on the quality and positiveness of these interactions.

In terms of power, foreign-born Hispanic women believe more strongly than Hispanic men or U.S.-born women that government programs favor African Americans. This belief may exacerbate feelings of competition between Hispanic and African American women, especially when considered in light of the current anti-immigrant climate in the United States. Adding to this sentiment is the view of foreign-born Hispanic women that immigrants do not take jobs from African Americans. This view can be interpreted as defensiveness and can fuel hostility between the groups.

A Feminist Approach to Understanding
Conflict between Women of Color

We now return to the statement made at the beginning of this chapter—that Black and Hispanic women hold more hostile attitudes toward each other's group than do their male counterparts. The findings of this study are provocative. It is almost inconceivable to imagine that African American and Hispanic women's attitudes toward each other's groups shape current and future negative relations between Hispanics and African Americans. Indeed, when we began telling our colleagues and students the results of the gender analyses, they universally expressed surprise. These findings seem counterintuitive. In the first place, men are perceived as more aggressive than women. Furthermore, women have in common the experience of being oppressed. They are oppressed by society at large and within their own ethnic-racial communities. Also, women of color are overrepresented among persons in poverty. Intuitively, then, it seems that this shared experience would lead to empathy, not hostility. How can we explain that women are more hostile toward other groups than men?

A clue is found in responses to a question dealing with identity. When students were asked to indicate which factor—gender, race-ethnicity, social class, or sexual orientation—has the most impact on their lives, the following responses were given. White women invariably responded that their gender most affects their lives. White men pointed to social class.

Black and Hispanic men almost always pointed to race. Black and Hispanic women, however, typically said that they cannot separate the impact of race and gender in their lives. Black and Hispanic women who are raised in poverty said that social class, race-ethnicity, and gender are inseparable. This inseparable intersection of identities is central to the feminists of color approach to understanding the lives of women of color. For feminists, the personal is political; women's consciousness is shaped by their experience in the society (Gilkes 1994). Hispanic and African American women's attitudes, beliefs, and feelings about members of other racial-ethnic groups can only be understood in the context of their day-to-day collective experiences of racism, sexism, and classism.

Unfortunately, we can only speculate about how the interactive realities of racism, classism, and sexism contribute to Hispanic and African American women's attitudes toward each other. As further analyses confirmed our preliminary findings that women are more hostile to other racial-ethnic groups than are men, we were left with the need to explain our findings without supporting data. For instance, we had no questions in our survey about relations between men and women or about gender roles within the family.

Nevertheless, we agree with the feminist of color perspective. We therefore draw on this literature, especially that written by Hispanic and Black women, and on social psychological literature on intergroup relations to speculate about what may explain women's greater intergroup hostility. In the sections that follow, the findings regarding conflict, prejudice, discrimination, power, fear, competition for jobs, Anglo favoritism, opportunities for government programs, impact of immigrants, amount of interaction, and overall relations between the groups are discussed in this broader feminist context. To facilitate understanding, we separate our discussion of classism, sexism, and racism, knowing, however, that these "isms" function interactively in women's lives. For instance, lower social class is correlated with ethnic-racial minority status, so racism and classism integrate. Further, being female is also correlated with lower social class status, so sexism and classism integrate. Finally, women of color are overrepresented among the lower social class, so race, class, and gender interact to form women's realities.

Classism

I'm getting tired of giving all my money to welfare and basically the Mexicans and Hispanics are the ones that are on welfare. Yes, true enough, my Black people are on welfare, you know, it's a lot of Black girls that are young, but they only have one or two [children], they don't pop one every year [like Mexicans].

AFRICAN AMERICAN FEMALE

The most obvious explanation for perceptions of poor relations between Hispanic and African American women involves competition for resources between members of the lower socioeconomic classes in both racial-ethnic groups. Poverty is not only the precursor for many negative quality of life concerns, it also contributes to feelings of hopelessness, low self-esteem, and a sense of loss of control (Nyamathi and Vasquez 1995). When people are struggling for economic survival, every penny counts. If there is a perception that another group is usurping funds that could go to their children or that another group is getting more opportunities than theirs, people cannot feel good about that group. The very survival of their family is at stake.

Our findings indicate that groups perceive competition for resources. Intergroup threat and conflict increase as perceived competition for resources increases between groups (Esses, Jackson, and Armstrong 1998). The greater the intergroup threat and conflict, the more hostility is expressed toward the source of the threat. This hostility helps to justify the conflict and the unfavorable treatment of out-group members. When competition over resources is present, proximity and contact increase intergroup hostility rather than decrease it. Importantly, it is perceived competition for resources that matters, not actual competition. In their roles as primary nurturers, Black and Hispanic women are particularly vulnerable to feelings of competitiveness as a means of protecting their children and other family members.

Consider the treatment of Hispanic women by African American women in locations that provide services to the poor. This treatment is not surprising given that African American women believe that immigrants are taking jobs from their group and that Hispanics are prejudiced against and fear them. The example of the hungry child is also indicative of lower social class experience. For these women, Hispanics are taking away resources that could be directed to their own families. Hostility is the understandable result.

However, as noted in chapter 3, our data indicate that with respect to foreign-born Hispanics, there are no statistically significant differences in attitudes between those with high or low levels of education or income. Both groups agreed or disagreed with the items in the same relative direction. There are more differences in attitudes between Hispanics and African Americans than between the social classes in either of those groups. However, as the economic disparity between social class groups increases, hostility between Hispanic and African American women and hence their children will probably increase. It is likely, then, that social class is a salient force that shapes intergroup perceptions. However, poverty is integrally entwined with racism and sexism. Hispanics and African Americans, in particular, women of these groups, are overrepresented among the poverty classes in proportion to their populations. Thus racism and sexism set up experiences of poverty and competition.

Racism

The centrality of African American women's community work points to the need to examine the importance of women in any community resisting racial oppression (Gilkes 1994, 242).

In short, status illegitimacy makes both high and low status group members aware of a variety of alternatives to the existing status structure, which may have the potential to produce intergroup conflict (Bettencourt and Bartholow 1998, 762).

Hierarchical and Colonized Status

Social class issues are entwined with hierarchical status, which in the United States cannot be separated from race and gender. Of race, social class, and gender, however, for African American and Hispanic women, the interaction of gender with race-ethnicity seems to be the most difficult to overcome. Racism sets up a social structure that situates Blacks and Hispanics according to their skin color and heritage of colonization. That hierarchy affords each ethnic-racial group a relative status and accompanying power. The privileges entailed in this power are representative voices in government, industry, education, financing, and health systems, and, in general, in all policies and processes that affect people's quality of life. As a result of having these privileges, a group's hierarchical, race-based status is legitimized. In the United States, White males are clearly at the top of the hierarchy, compared to people of color and women. Hispanic and African American women receive what is left after the top group's needs are met, setting up competition for legitimized status on the next rung of the social ladder.

A history of colonized status determines in part a group's place in the social hierarchy. Hispanic and African American women have experienced colonization: African Americans were enslaved, and Mexican Americans were colonized on their own land after the U.S.–Mexican war. The vestiges of this colonization remain today, further marginalizing Hispanic and Black women. The experience of being marginalized includes feelings of victimization, self-denial, assimilation, strong ambivalence, and a fundamental need for change (Comas-Díaz 1994). Minority women live in borderlands—caught between worlds (Anzaldúa 1987). They do not entirely fit in with the mainstream White culture or with their mother culture (Anzaldúa 1987). Women of color respond to this lack of belonging with feelings of alienation and self-defense of their families, communities, and ethnic group as a whole. This self-defense is exemplified by attitudes such as "Blacks are good, Mexicans are bad" and "us versus them." These reactions set up intergroup competition and conflict and stress group differences. They do not readily allow for Hispanic and African American women's unity with or empathy for each other. The women's focus is on their own group's survival. As a result, this "us versus them" survival attitude, which emphasizes intergroup differences, is passed on to their children, thus affecting intergroup relations.

Which group has higher status, African Americans or Hispanics? As indicated above, Hispanic women believe that Anglos favor African Americans. Since Whites occupy the top of the power hierarchy, their favor would contribute to a group's status. Hispanic women also believe that African Americans have too much power, which is correlated with status. Anti-immigrant legislation most assuredly has contributed to Hispanics', especially foreign-born Hispanics', perceptions that Blacks have more power than they do. In addition, African Americans have more political power than do U.S.-born Hispanics (Delgado 1999). As a group, African Americans vote more consistently than Hispanics (see chap. 5), so politicians have historically catered more to Blacks.[2] Taken together, this information leads to the impression that African Americans have higher status than do Hispanics, especially the foreign born. However, it is unlikely that Hispanic women accept this higher status of African Americans as legitimate.

Status legitimacy is the extent to which both high- and low-status groups accept the validity of a status. When the status structure is perceived as illegitimate, the situation conflicts with superordinate values of justice, fairness, or equity. Group members become cognitively aware of alternatives to the existing social order. Low-status groups become more biased in their intergroup attitudes. Such a context might explain Hispanic women's hostility to African Americans.

When status is considered legitimate, high-status groups are more biased than low-status groups (Bettencourt and Bartholow 1998). Recall that African Americans believe that Hispanics are benefiting from Blacks' civil rights struggles. African Americans may believe that they have earned any status they have as a result of their continuing struggles. Such a perception of status legitimacy would explain Black women's hostile reactions to Hispanics.

Cultural Differences

Prejudice may derive in part from the perception that a group fails to support one's values, and the most consensually derogated out-groups are likely to be widely perceived as violating many important values (Biernat et al. 1996, 184). If the stereotypes of any group suggest that members do not uphold a particular value, then an individual's endorsement of that value will predict rejection of members of that out-group (Biernat et al. 1996, 155).

Another function of racism is to devalue cultural differences. As members of U.S. society, Black and Hispanic women may internalize the racist ideology that if a group is different from us in some way, that difference must be bad or must be responsible for our group's negative experiences. Devaluing group differences implies acceptance of generalized standards of behavior and attitudes, which in turn implies a universal standard of excellence.

Given their common experience of socialization in the United States, it is likely that U.S.-born Hispanic women share more generalized standards or cultural values with African American women than do their foreign-born counterparts. Most important, because the foreign born are generally closer to their cultural heritage than the U.S.-born Hispanics, the former holds more traditionally conservative cultural values than the latter. Our research findings confirm these cultural differences (see chap. 5).

For instance, cultural values of Hispanics include *respeto* and humility (Díaz-Guerrero 1987). African Americans also share these values, but they are not as stereotypically associated with African Americans as they are with Hispanics. Therefore, Hispanics who are personally unfamiliar with African Americans may not realize that they share these values.

For example, the media often portray African Americans as engaging in boasting, the opposite of humility. Although African Americans tend to engage in boasting, it is done as a form of humor, which may be mis-interpreted by Hispanics (Kochman 1987). Indeed, our findings indicate that Hispanics believe that African Americans speak loudly, are unman-nerly, and are egotistical (see chap. 2). These behaviors seem to be part of Hispanics' collective knowledge about African Americans. Hispanic women very likely pass on this negatively biased information about Afri-can Americans to their children, increasing perceptions of vast differences between the groups.

In addition, Hispanics believe more than do African Americans that their children who work should contribute to the family income (see chap. 3). This finding is consistent with existing literature that concludes that Mexicans emphasize affiliative interdependent relationships between parents and children (Díaz-Guerrero and Szalay 1993) and that Mexican adolescents are more traditional than bicultural (Rodriguez, Ramirez, and Korman 1999) and possess the culturally inculcated Hispanic virtues of obedience, patience, and self-abnegation. Other findings of cultural differences indicate that Hispanics are more opposed to abortion than are African Americans (see chap. 3). Hispanics also see themselves as more group oriented, compared to African Americans. When Hispanics believe that African Americans do not share these traditional norms, their chil-dren also learn that "Blacks are different." In a racist society, "different" equals "bad."

African Americans are uncomfortable with the Spanish language. Lan-guage differences are probably the most obvious representation of group differences. For the past decade in the United States, there has been a strong anti-bilingual education, English-only movement. This move-ment lends credence to the perception that speaking Spanish is bad or "un-American" and justifies African American women's sentiments against speaking Spanish and against those who do speak Spanish.

The findings presented here are also consistent with observations of differences in Hispanic and Black women's cultural values reported by researchers at the University of Texas School of Public Health in Hous-ton (Mullen, pers. com. 1995). Some of these researchers have noted that Hispanic women are not receiving necessary health care benefits, such as yearly gynecological exams and prenatal care. In informal surveys with the medical school personnel, Hispanic women indicate that they are in-timidated by Black clinic workers, who, they say, speak loudly, rudely, and generally disrespectfully. The women state that they would rather do without health care for themselves and, in some cases, for their children than put up with what they perceive as poor treatment from Black clinic workers. These perceptions of rudeness may be rooted in cultural differences in values of appropriate communication styles for women. Hispanic women are traditionally socialized to behave conservatively. Black women, however, are members of a matriarchal culture that facilitates more assertive behavior than that typically found in traditionally patriarchal Hispanic women's cultures. This interaction speaks to the importance of perceived values and interpretation. Effective relationships may be promoted by considering multicultural values and experiences (Biernat et al. 1996; Díaz-Loving and Draguns 1999). Therefore, training that includes such values can facilitate intergroup respect and relations. As Hughes states, "The important question society needs to address concerns how to teach our children to appreciate difference and value diversity in ways that adults have not" (1997, 123).

In any event, it is highly likely that Hispanic children observe the negative interactions between their mothers and African American women. As a result, Hispanic children are learning anti-Black attitudes both from personal observation and from their mothers. African American children learn anti-Hispanic attitudes vicariously from observing their mothers' behaviors and from hearing mothers' conversations about race-related work experiences.

This situation is an excellent example of how the personal is political. It does not matter to Hispanic women why African American women behave in this manner. It just matters that this behavior affects their children's and their own lives. Nor does it matter to African American women that Hispanics perceive them as rude. What matters is the perception that Hispanics who may not belong in this country are taking resources that could otherwise be channeled to their group.

Sexism

Gender oppression combines with what Root (1992) describes as insidious trauma, which interacts with racism and poverty. Hispanic and African American women's exposure to this trauma activates survival behaviors and feelings of alienation. When women are struggling for their own and their families' survival, helping members of other racial-ethnic groups survive is not a priority or part of their conscious thought. Furthermore, given the role of societal oppression in their own experiences within their families, it is very likely that women's survival strategies and displaced aggression, wittingly or unwittingly, encompass hostility to out-group members and defense of their own communities. Following are some examples of the manifestations of sexism that may lead to feelings of alienation and hostility to anyone who is not a trusted confidant, especially members of other ethnic-racial groups.

Sexism and Poverty

Perhaps the most pervasive form of sexism is manifested in women's economic status. Black and Hispanic women are likely to be paid less than men of any ethnic-racial group and less than White women (Thomas, Herring, and Horton 1995). Black and Hispanic women are less likely than men or White women to have a formal education. When they do have college degrees, they have fewer returns from their education than do men and White women (Thomas, Herring, and Horton 1995). Women's lower economic power is related to poor health outcomes and prevention, including higher infant mortality (Davis 1995), higher exposure to crime, including murder (Rolison and Keith 1995), and unsafe housing, including exposure to environmental hazards (Rogers 1995).

Sexualized Racial Identities

Hispanic and African American women are particularly vulnerable to being racially objectified as exotic sex objects. For instance, during slavery, Black women were consistently used as sex objects by their owners. More recently, Black women who report being raped are likely to be seen as deserving or wanting it, by virtue of a stereotypical inherent sexuality associated with Black women. Hispanic women are viewed as "hot" objects looking for sexual favors. For Hispanic and African American women, then, race intersects with gender such that "the status of being colonized involves the added negation of their individuality by their being subjected to sexual-racial objectification. Women of color are stripped of their humanity, denied their individuality, and devalued" (Comas-Díaz 1994, 289).

Family Violence

The loss of a sense of dignity and respect in the macho breeds a false machismo which leads [men] to put down women and even to brutalize them (Anzaldúa 1990, 383).

Women and children then become suitable recipients for the displaced anger of oppressed men (Espín 1994, 266).

Women of color are also subject to oppression in their families (Espín 1994; Root 1992). As White upper-middle-class opportunities and standards that are unattainable define manhood for most men of color, their expressions of manhood become distorted. Some Hispanic and African American men assert their domination and masculinity in the territory of personal relationships and family, resulting in women's experiences of domestic violence, incest, and sexual abuse (Flores-Ortiz 1993, 1997; Rodriguez 1997; Romero and Wyatt 1999).

Summary

Hispanic and African American women's typical responses to racial-sexual objectification and to the violence in their homes is to remain silent and nontrusting of anyone, including social service or mental health workers (Flores-Ortiz 1993, 1997; Rodriguez 1997; Romero and Wyatt 1999). Furthermore, Hispanic and African American women often lack the economic power to take action against their aggressors. Consequently, women's feelings of anger and hostility generally remain unresolved, and women are likely to displace their anger and hostility onto others, especially members of other ethnic groups who may be perceived as contributing to their negative life experiences.

Developing a Critical Consciousness

Let us be clear that the findings in this survey do not suggest that women alone are to blame for existing or future poor intergroup relations. Indeed, women function in a patriarchal society. Further, men are not exempt from the responsibility of intergroup relations, as both men and women shape their children's attitudes and the environment in which they live. What these data do suggest is that women may have to reframe their intergroup attitudes and take a leadership role in shaping intergroup relations.

In the 1970s many feminists of color favored coalitions between their groups, while keeping their respective autonomous organizations (Garcia 1989, 232). For the sake of their children's future, it is time to renew this call for unity among women of color.

However, the early history of the women's suffrage movement set the stage for the schism, conflict, and hostility between Hispanic and African American women today. Because White women often did not support equal rights for men and women of color, it is difficult for women of color to trust that members of other groups will support their causes. Historically, the women's movement was so centered on White middle-class women that women of color wondered, "rights for which women?" (Cotera 1997, 224). Later, during the feminist movement of the 1960s and 1970s, issues of race and class continued to be put aside. Moreover, Black and Hispanic women have sought to end sexist oppression within a broader nationalist struggle to end racist oppression (Davis 1983; Dill 1983). However, the women have been criticized for threatening solidarity with men (Garcia 1989; hooks 1984; Pesquera and Segura 1993). Today the White women's movement places more emphasis on the plight of women in third world countries. However, this feminist movement seems to continue to ignore the third world conditions in the United States under which some Hispanic and African American women reside and work. Therefore, although women interact more than their male counterparts, as indicated in our findings, these interactions are mired in a history of distrust and competition and survival strategies within the group.

Hispanic and African American women can promote positive relations between their groups by emphasizing the common experiences of racism and discrimination in the United States. This commonality can foster acts of resistance and cooperation based on a shared history of dispossession, prejudice, discrimination, and immigration (Ochoa 1999). Hispanic and African American women's critical consciousness will facilitate feelings of empathy for each other's group. Empathy in various forms can play an important role in combating prejudice and improving intergroup relations (Stephan and Finlay 1999). Cognitive empathy leads people to see that they are less different from other groups than they thought. Empathizing with people who are suffering leads to concern, or reactive empathy. Reactive empathy leads to parallel empathy, which facilitates attitude change by arousing feelings of injustice (Stephan and Finlay 1999). Empathy as a means to form closer relations is consistent with the creation of a common, superordinate identity. Hispanics and African Americans may form a common identity as historically oppressed groups and survivors who can join together to fight societal discrimination against their members (see chap. 6 for a fuller discussion of this argument). A greater awareness among women of color will facilitate

Hispanic and African American women's understanding of their group's common cultural values and social status. This understanding will facilitate passing on to their children more positive intergroup opinions and a united front against continued oppression against both groups. As feminist scholars state, "Diversity among women of color creates a tension between what connects them and what separates them. Women of color share commonalties with other groups of women. The challenge therefore is to build upon the connections while recognizing the differences. However, this challenge remains unfulfilled" (Comas-Díaz and Greene 1994, 342).

Notes

1. Questionnaire: As explained in chapter 1, items for the survey results reported here were adapted from research on intergroup relations. Items tapped into perceptions of conflict and attitudes that may give rise to hostility between Hispanics and African Americans. Most responses were provided on a Likert-type scale anchored with 1 (strongly disagree) and 5 (strongly agree). Other responses were tailored specifically to the item. Items are listed in tables 4.1–4.5. Analyses: Mean differences between groups were compared for statistical significance. Statistical significance means that the probability that these findings occurred by random chance alone is less than 5 out of 100 ($p < .05$). In other words, statistical significance indicates that there is a relationship between racial attitudes and comparison group membership.

2. However, that situation may be changing. At the Republican National Convention of 2000, then Republican presidential nominee, George W. Bush, openly courted Hispanics.

Chapter 5

Areas of Agreement

We can get along with anybody. We have a long history of having
to get along with everybody.

Fifty-three-year-old Black male

Of course we can get along. All we have to do is put our differences aside and work on things that are common to both groups.
What we have in common far outweighs our differences and we
need to realize this and start moving forward together.

Thirty-two-year-old Hispanic female

As in all social relationships, there are issues that provoke disagreement
and issues on which there is consensus. Conflict can be so severe that
it prevents relationships from continuing or even forming. Fortunately,
this is not the situation for Hispanics and African Americans in Houston.

There are many similarities between Hispanics and African Americans that can and do serve as a basis not only for consensus but also
for cooperation and coalition building. Mexican Americans and African
Americans became residents in the United States through force. Both
groups are physically and culturally different from Anglo-Americans.
Both groups have experienced and continue to experience discrimination in all spheres of American life: education, employment, income,
housing, health care, and life chances. Both groups have large numbers
of poor people in their communities, and both groups have a history of
struggling to gain parity and justice in the United States. In sum, African Americans and Hispanics are subordinate minority groups who share
common views on a variety of subjects. Agreement does not necessarily
mean consensus on all facets of an issue, nor does it mean agreement
when the opinions of African Americans and Hispanics are investigated
at a different level of analysis, such as the state or national level. What

follows is an examination of the commonly held views as they surfaced in the Black-Brown survey in Houston.

Views Held in Common by African Americans and Hispanics

Prayer in Public Schools

The issue of prayer in the public schools can be framed along a conservative-liberal continuum. Conservatives support prayer in public schools and believe that elimination of religion in the public school system has led to many of the nation's social problems. Before 1963, when the U.S. Supreme Court ruled in *Abington v. Schempp* (374 U.S. 203) that prayer in public schools was unconstitutional, each school day started with the Pledge of Allegiance and the recital of the Lord's Prayer. A change in this practice was prompted by liberals who believe that school prayer violates the constitutional mandate of separation of church and state and that it imposes Christian beliefs and practices on non-Christians. By large majorities, Hispanics and African Americans in the Black-Brown survey side with conservatives on the issue and support prayer in public schools (table 5.1).

This support is not surprising as a majority of Hispanics and Blacks in Houston state that religion is very important in their lives (Klineberg 1999). At the national level, surveys show that there is mixed support by Hispanics and Blacks for school prayer, depending on how and when the question is asked. When asked in a 1997 survey if organized prayer in school is the kind of issue for which the Constitution should be changed, 59 percent of African Americans and 67 percent of Hispanics said yes (CBS News, *New York Times* Poll, January 19, 1997). However, in a 1996 survey question that asked if they would approve or disapprove of mandatory prayer in schools as a way to improve the country's moral climate, 44 percent of African Americans compared to 17 percent of Hispanics said they would approve (*Time,* CNN, Yankelovich, July 1996). Also, in 1995, when asked how high a priority Congress should give to a constitutional amendment to allow prayer in school, 61 percent of African Americans said it should be top or high priority, compared to 44 percent of Hispanics (Gallup, CNN, *USA Today* Poll, January 1995).

In all but one of the surveys cited, including the Black-Brown survey in Houston, more African Americans than Hispanics expressed support for prayer in public schools, regardless of how the question was framed.

Table 5.1 Questions That Elicit Similar Responses among Blacks and U.S.- and Foreign-born Hispanics

| | % AGREE | | |
| | U.S.-BORN HISPANICS | FOREIGN-BORN HISPANICS | AFRICAN AMERICANS |
QUESTIONS			
Prayer should be allowed in public schools.	70	73	88
Homosexuals should be allowed to do what they want to do as long as they don't hurt other people.	68	73	64
Government should do more to help the poor and disadvantaged.	75	85	86
People should not receive welfare for more than two years.	70	50	50
Teenage women who have children out of wedlock should not be eligible for welfare.	37	35	24
Relatives are more important than friends.	86	81	73
It is more important to take care of your family's needs than it is to take care of your personal needs.	81	81	74
Minority group parents should attempt to maintain their ethnic identity and pass that on to their children.	90	92	91
It is a good idea for a person to have friends from different cultures.	96	95	94
In order to prevent undocumented immigrants from entering the labor force, everyone in the U.S. should be required to carry a national identification card.	56	56	65
People can overcome the disadvantages of discrimination if they try hard enough.	86	83	72
African Americans fear Hispanics.	14	18	8
Most Hispanics are prejudiced against African Americans.	24	35	36
Hispanics have too much power.	5	17	13
Hispanics are members of the White race.	24	40	15

Why? It may have to do with the fact that the majority of African Americans are Protestants and the majority of Hispanics are Catholic. Protestants have made more of the issue than have Catholics. Also, historically, religion has been more important to the survival of African Americans and the church has been and continues to be more active in the political affairs of the African American community.

Homosexuality and Lifestyle

Legislating civil rights for gays and lesbians has become increasingly controversial in recent years. Conservative and religious groups oppose antidiscrimination protection of gays and lesbians. Many conservatives oppose same-sex marriage, health and other insurance benefits for homosexuals who live together, and gays and lesbians being employed in certain professions, such as teaching in elementary schools and the ministry. Liberal groups hold that homosexuals should be protected from discrimination, granted the same rights as other couples, and allowed to live whatever lifestyle they choose.

African Americans and Hispanics in the Black-Brown survey tend to share the liberal point of view and feel that homosexuals should be allowed to do what they want as long as they are not hurting other people. More of the foreign-born Hispanics feel this way than either U.S.-born Hispanics or African Americans (table 5.1).

Klineberg's (1999) Houston Area Survey also found support for equal civil rights for homosexuals, even though the majority of Hispanics and Blacks considered homosexuality morally wrong. Hispanics and Blacks may support equal treatment for gays and lesbians, despite their concerns on moral grounds, because they believe that homosexuals are being singled out for exclusionary practices, as have racial and ethnic minorities.

A national survey conducted by *Time* and CNN (October 16, 1998) shows that Hispanics are more tolerant of homosexuals than are African Americans on some specific issues: more Hispanics (79 percent) than African Americans (36 percent) do not think that homosexual relations are a moral issue; more Hispanics (36 percent) than African Americans (21 percent) think that homosexual marriages should be recognized by law; more Hispanics (42 percent) than African Americans (29 percent) think that homosexuals should be permitted to adopt children legally; more Hispanics (56 percent) than African Americans (44 percent) find the homosexual lifestyle acceptable but not for themselves; more Hispanics (60 percent) than African Americans (40 percent) would allow their children to watch a television program that had a homosexual character; and more Hispanics (27 percent) than African Americans (16 percent) do not think that homosexual rights get enough attention.

On several of the issues, less than a majority of Hispanics respond in support of gay and lesbian issues. Nevertheless, what is intriguing is that Hispanic culture is reportedly a macho culture that emphasizes male dominance and strict adherence to traditional gender roles, especially in regard to sexual behavior. Some observers say that male roles are so dominant that a tradition of phallic worship permeates the culture (Castillo 1994; Miranda 1997; Stavans 1996). These are norms that would not lead one to expect support for the rights of homosexuals. Although the results reported here do not absolutely contradict these norms, they nevertheless caution against rigid acceptance.

The national surveys cited do not distinguish between U.S.- and foreign-born Hispanics. Recall that the foreign born in the Black-Brown survey support homosexuals more than U.S.-born Hispanics and African Americans do. Given that foreign-born Hispanics are thought more likely than U.S.-born Hispanics to perpetuate traditional Hispanic culture and that traditional Hispanic culture is more homophobic than the syncretic culture of U.S.-born Hispanics, their greater support of homosexuals is noteworthy. It is intriguing to imagine gays, lesbians, and Hispanic immigrants forming a coalition for gay rights. Discrimination against gays and lesbians is emerging as the new civil rights issue and could be a divisive one for Hispanics and African Americans. In addition to not being as supportive, African Americans may begin to feel that an emphasis on civil rights for gays and lesbians detracts from their continuing struggle for civil rights.

Government Support and Welfare

A large majority of Hispanics and African Americans in the Black-Brown survey feel that government should do more to help the poor and disadvantaged (see table 5.1). This support is not surprising given that minorities have relied on the government, especially in recent years, to protect and ensure their opportunities and to help them combat discrimination. However, respondents believe there are limits as to how long government should help the disadvantaged. The majority of Hispanics and African Americans agree that people should not receive welfare for more than two years (see table 5.1). This sentiment is especially widespread among U.S.-born Hispanics. At the national level, at least one survey reported a similar finding (Princeton Survey Research, March 10, 1998). The survey asked respondents if poor people had become too dependent on government assistance programs. A large majority of Blacks and Hispanics agreed, but Hispanics agreed (77 percent) more than did African Americans (69 percent). More Hispanics (91 percent) than African Americans (83 percent) also believe that every able-bodied person should have to do some type of work to receive welfare or unemployment benefits, although the majorities in both groups are very large (NBC News, *Wall Street Journal Poll*, March 1999). Hispanics may feel this way because they do not depend on government assistance to the same degree as do African Americans (U.S. Census Bureau 1995). In addition, African Americans are more integrated than Hispanics into the public sector as employees and may feel more allegiance to government. In many instances the government employs African Americans to offset discrimination in the private sector.

A majority of the sample in the Black-Brown survey also believes that teenage women who have children out of wedlock should not be denied welfare (table 5.1). More African Americans than Hispanics feel this way. As noted in chapter 3, the higher rate of out-of-wedlock births among African Americans may explain their higher rates of support.

The issue of welfare is an emotional one. It carries with it many negative racial stereotypes and angry reactions, especially from African Americans who believe that welfare has been defined as a "black problem" (Kaiser Family Foundation, National Association of Black Journalists, 1998).

Family Values

The family is important to both groups. Both African Americans and Hispanics feel that relatives are more important than friends and that it is more important to take care of one's family's needs than one's personal needs (table 5.1). These types of questions can automatically elicit positive responses regardless of race. For example, Hispanics are considered a people with unusually strong family ties. However, the percentage of Hispanics who agree with the importance of the family is not significantly different from that of African Americans. One can infer that cultural beliefs about the family are equally strong in both groups. A majority of foreign-born Hispanics agree on the importance of relatives and taking care of family needs before personal needs, but they do not feel this way to the same extent as African Americans and U.S.-born Hispanics. This is not what one would expect from a foreign-born community whose culture is reportedly very family oriented. Perhaps migration has loosened the bonds. Some research has found that people who migrate from Mexico to the United States are risk takers and are not as attached to their families relative to people who do not migrate (Cornelius 1975).

Identity and Culture

Maintaining their ethnic identity and culture while at the same time wanting to associate with other racial-ethnic groups is important for Hispanics and African Americans. At least 90 percent of the respondents in each of the three groups in the Black-Brown survey agreed that maintaining their ethnic identity is important (table 5.1). Complete assimilation into Anglo-American culture at the expense of losing their own culture does not seem a desirable goal. This is the sentiment underlying the nationalistic feelings so often expressed in terms of self-determination and advocacy of multiculturalism (Gordon and Newfield 1997). Multiculturalism is one of the ways in which people of color elevate, protect, and foster pride in cultures that traditionally have been attacked.

The desire for a multicultural society may also explain why Hispanic and African American respondents say that it is good to have friends from different cultures. Perhaps these sentiments acknowledge the value found in being exposed to cultural diversity and the right to live and mingle with other groups. Hispanics and African Americans, after all, are usually in the forefront of the cultural diversity movement in U.S. society. However, as noted in Chapter 3, there appears to be a limit to the level of intimacy in which Hispanics and African Americans are willing to engage.

Undocumented Immigration

To discourage undocumented immigrants from coming to the United States, some groups have advocated a national identification card that every citizen and legal resident would be required to carry and present at the time of employment. The intention is to prevent immigrants who are in the United States without authorization from entering the labor market. Knowing that one needs a national identification card to work presumably would discourage illegal immigration. Many people oppose the idea because it unfairly singles out Mexicans, as they comprise the largest group who are in the United States without proper documentation (Hagan, Rodriguez, and Capps 1999).

Most Hispanics and African Americans in the Black-Brown survey, but especially African Americans, support the idea of a national identification card (table 5.1). The support expressed by African Americans is not surprising as many perceive immigrants as an economic threat. In the Black-Brown survey, support for a national identification card is especially strong among low-income, poorly educated African American females, again reflecting the greater anti-immigrant sentiment among African American women reported earlier. Among U.S.-born Hispanics, it is the poorly educated who express the greatest support for a national identification card; they may also perceive immigrants as an economic threat.

A majority of Hispanic immigrants support a mandatory national identification card. One would not expect this result, as it could cause undue hardships for fellow immigrants—hardships they may have endured themselves. Perhaps most of the immigrants in the sample entered the United States legally or have legalized their status and therefore do not identify with the undocumented; having a national identification card could help to differentiate legal immigrants from the undocumented. Or it could be that they see undocumented immigrants as a source of economic competition. Generally, undocumented workers earn less than immigrants who are in the United States legally (Phillips and Massey 1999; Tienda and Singer 1995). Perhaps immigrants perceive undocumented workers as the source of social problems in the barrios and the perpetuators of negative stereotypes. Or it may be that there is an unrealistic expectation of unity among immigrants. Whatever the reason, the support for a national identification card among foreign-born Hispanics is a significant finding.

Race Relations

African Americans and Hispanics agree that discrimination can be overcome if one tries hard enough (table 5.1). This finding is consistent with Klineberg's (1999) findings that Hispanics and African Americans feel they experience discrimination in Houston quite often. If there is a belief that discrimination can be overcome, then perhaps the degree of discrimination is not severe, or it could mean that regardless of how difficult the discriminatory barriers may be, there is a persistence and determination to overcome them.

There is widespread agreement that African Americans do not fear Hispanics (table 5.1). As pointed out earlier, fear is an important component of race relations. It is not known, of course, how the respondents interpreted the term "fear," but it is assumed that it is not fear rooted in economic circumstances, since many African Americans see immigrants as an economic threat. African Americans may have interpreted "fear" as meaning physical fear. Regardless of how the term was interpreted, a large majority of the respondents agree that African Americans do not fear Hispanics.

Also, a majority of each group do not believe that Hispanics are prejudiced against African Americans (table 5.1). This finding bodes well for intergroup relations.

About one-third of African Americans and foreign-born Hispanics in the Black-Brown survey feel that Hispanics are prejudiced against African Americans. Within the foreign-born sample, it tends to be females who feel this way. This again raises the question, what shapes the views of the foreign born given that they do not have extensive contact with African Americans? Are they aware that some African Americans do not welcome them to the United States? Have they been socialized into the anti-Black feelings endemic in American culture? Have they assimilated the negative images of African Americans portrayed in the media?

African Americans who believe that Hispanics are prejudiced against them may believe that everyone is prejudiced against them. Perhaps they know that Hispanics fear them and interpret this fear as prejudice. This belief may result from anti-Black sentiments and stereotypes that are an integral part of the culture. There is also agreement that Hispanics do not have too much power (table 5.1). Given that Hispanics only recently have become a significant segment of the population in the United States, that power is generally associated with voting and political representation, and that Hispanics lag behind African Americans in both areas, it is not surprising that there is a perception that Hispanics do not have too much power. Is this why many African Americans say they do not fear Hispanics?

A majority of the respondents in the Black-Brown survey do not believe that Hispanics are members of the "White race" (table 5.1). This question was included in the survey for two reasons. First, the skin color of Hispanics ranges from very fair and Anglo-looking to very dark, Indian, and mulatto in appearance. Thus some Hispanics believe that they are members of the Caucasian or White race. Second, at one time Hispanics were legally declared a special category of White people (De Leon 1993). Hispanics fought this designation after the U.S. Supreme

Court ruled that the segregation of Blacks and Anglos in the public school system was unconstitutional. School districts in Texas subsequently started busing African Americans to Hispanic schools and vice versa under the premise that Hispanics were legally "White" (San Miguel 2001).

There are two findings shown in table 5.1 that are caveats to the discussion above. First, more African Americans than U.S.- and foreign-born Hispanics do not believe that Hispanics are members of the White race. This sentiment is greatest among better-educated African Americans. African Americans, because of their experiences in the United States, may have a greater awareness of what constitutes "Whiteness" in America and thus simply do not believe that Hispanics are "White." Second, 40 percent of the foreign born agree that Hispanics are indeed White, a belief that is especially apparent among those with the lowest level of educational attainment. Defining or perceiving oneself as White may make one feel that she or he has a higher social status than is the case, or it could be an acknowledgment of White privilege. Knowing that African Americans and Hispanics rank at the lower end of the racial hierarchy may lead some foreign-born Hispanics to grasp at whatever they can to distinguish themselves from African Americans.

Working Together

When asked how they would characterize relations between Hispanics and African Americans in Houston, 80 percent of U.S.-born Hispanics, 74 percent of African Americans, and 66 percent of foreign-born Hispanics in the Black-Brown survey defined them as either somewhat good or very good. Two points should be noted. First, although a majority of foreign-born Hispanics defined the relationship as positive, fewer did so in comparison to U.S.-born Hispanics and African Americans. This is in line with the more negative perceptions that the foreign born have of African Americans. Second, how does one reconcile the positive evaluation with the perceptions of conflict reported in chapter 3? How can people say that the relationship between African Americans and Hispanics is good and also perceive conflict between them? It could be that the intensity of conflict is not perceived as serious and that on balance the positive aspects of the relationship outweigh the negative aspects. Or it could be that general questions, such as the ones asked in the survey, elicit general positive responses, whereas specific questions, such as those dealing with immigration and the speaking of Spanish in the workplace, tend to generate more accurate responses. Regardless, this is a contradiction that needs further examination.

Future Relations

When asked what one issue the respondents believed Hispanics and African Americans could work on together, education, discrimination, and getting along, in that order, were the issues most often cited. It is not surprising that education ranked as the top issue since reducing the drop-out rate, increasing the number of college graduates, and improving the quality of educational services have long been goals of advocacy groups in both communities. Likewise, both groups have a long history of fighting discriminatory barriers not only in education but in other areas as well, such as employment, housing, politics, and health care. Getting along, again, speaks to the perception that there is room for improvement in the relationship between African Americans and Hispanics, especially because both groups will encounter each other more and more often in Houston and other major cities of the United States.

Political Efficacy: Consensus and Conflict

For the most part, Hispanics and African Americans have a history of cooperating and forming coalitions in the political arena. They have supported each other's candidates and formed coalitions in support of common concerns on the city council, on the school board, and in the state legislature. African Americans and Hispanics also tend to vote for Democrats. In the 2000 presidential election, for example, both groups in Houston supported Vice President Al Gore over Texas governor George W. Bush. There have been instances of conflict, however, that usually occur when a Hispanic or an African American is seeking the same elected or appointed office. Also, there have been instances in which Anglo candidates have been able to divide Hispanic voters and as a result cause strain between African Americans and Hispanics. In recent mayoral elections, for example, Anglo candidates have been successful in garnering a majority or a large percentage of the Hispanic vote in races against African American candidates. In one instance the Anglo candidate, Bob Lanier, won, and more recently the African American candidate, Lee P. Brown, won.

In the most recent mayoral election a Hispanic Cuban, Orlando Sanchez, faced incumbent Lee P. Brown, the city's first African American mayor, in a runoff election. The race was significant because it pitted a well-financed Hispanic candidate against a well-financed African American incumbent, the first time in Houston's history that the major candidates for mayor were minorities. Sanchez lost the race but in the process galvanized the Hispanic vote and increased the turnout of Hispanic voters. The race may signal the emergence of Hispanics as a major electoral force in Houston.

Relative Political Influence

African Americans are the second most influential group of voters in Houston, ranking behind Anglos. Hispanics born in the United States rank a distant third, and the number of naturalized immigrants who vote is small. In citywide elections African Americans make up approximately 28 percent of the electorate and U.S.-born Hispanics make up about 12 percent. There are no estimates available for the number of naturalized Hispanic immigrants who vote in citywide elections, but in recent exit polls in single member districts, the number of Hispanic voters who indicate that they are naturalized immigrants has never exceeded 19 percent of the total Hispanic vote (Mindiola 1992; Mindiola and Santos 1999).

African American voters are influential not only because of their numbers but also because of their discipline and bloc voting. Two examples illustrate these characteristics. In 1997 a referendum concerning affirmative action was on the ballot in conjunction with a mayoral election in which an African American was running against a wealthy Anglo. The African American turnout jumped from 28 percent, the normal rate, to 35 percent. This impressive increase reflects intense motivation. In terms of how their votes were cast, 93 percent voted to keep affirmative action. Without the African American vote, the Anglo candidate would have won the election and the city's affirmative action program would have been eliminated. The second example is the 2001 runoff election mentioned above. In response to the serious challenge Brown faced from Sanchez, the African American vote increased to approximately 33 percent of the total votes cast and 95 percent of African American votes went to Brown. Again, without this impressive display of numbers and solidarity, Brown would have lost the election.

In 2001 there were twenty-four African American elected officials in Houston. This includes the first African American mayor of the city, who was elected in 1997, and one congresswoman, who is the fourth African American from Houston to serve in Congress. In contrast, there are eigh-

Table 5.2 Political Efficacy Questions

	U.S.-BORN HISPANICS	% AGREE FOREIGN-BORN HISPANICS	AFRICAN AMERICANS
I consider myself to be well qualified to participate in politics.	43	25	58
I feel that I have a pretty good understanding of the important issues facing our country.	83	74	83
I feel that I could do as good a job in public office as most other people.	70	47	70
I think that I am better informed about politics and government than most people.	46	35	51
Sometimes politics and government seem so complicated that a person like me can't really understand what is going on.	58	66	55
I don't think public officials care much what people like me think.	65	54	71

teen elected Hispanic officials in Houston and there has never been a Hispanic mayor or a Hispanic elected to Congress from the Houston area.

In terms of party affiliation, Hispanics are more diverse than African Americans. U.S.-born Hispanics identify their political party affiliation as follows: 39 percent Democrat, 19 percent Republican, 30 percent Independent or Other, and 12 percent no affiliation. Among Hispanic immigrants, 23 percent say they are Democrat, 7 percent Republican, 26 percent Independent or Other, and 45 percent no affiliation. African Americans are more monolithic in their party affiliation, with 68 percent identifying themselves as Democrats, 3 percent Republican, 24 percent Independent or Other, and 5 percent no affiliation.

The responses to six questions dealing with political efficacy reveal the hierarchy of political influence in Houston among African Americans and Hispanics (table 5.2). "Political efficacy" refers to the belief that one's participation in the political process is meaningful and influential and makes a difference. In other words, it refers to feelings of political empowerment. Political efficacy scores range from an average of 1, indicating a low level, to 5, indicating a high level. The average efficacy score for African Americans is 3.6, compared to 3.22 for U.S.-born Hispanics and 2.8 for foreign-born Hispanics. Within each group the segments that tend to feel more political empowerment are the young, better-educated, high-income males—segments of the population that tend to be active in community affairs.

Given the political success that African Americans have experienced in Houston, it is not surprising that they feel more politically empowered in comparison to Hispanics. Note in table 5.2, however, that all three groups, but especially African Americans, agree in large numbers that public officials do not care about what "people like me think." Thus, although African Americans may feel more politically empowered, there is still some skepticism that their voices are being heeded.

It is not surprising that the foreign born feel more alienated from the political process. The majority are monolingual Spanish speakers and are not citizens. However, it is striking that 57 percent of Hispanic immigrants have either a Democratic, Republican, or Independent political identity. Although foreign-born Hispanics may not be able to vote, a majority have nevertheless been integrated into the political system enough to assume an American political identity. Integration into the American political system is also suggested by political efficacy scores: 3.0 for immigrants who say they have a political party identity, compared to 2.5 for immigrants who say they do not know their party affiliation.

Further, among those who express a political party affiliation, Republicans have a higher political efficacy score than Democrats or Independents: 3.8, 3.1, and 3.0, respectively. Note that the political efficacy score for immigrants who identify as Republicans is slightly higher than that for African Americans, which is 3.6. Also, as might be expected, age, length of time in the United States, and facility in the English language play a role in fostering political integration, as immigrants who have a political party affiliation are older and have been in the United States longer. The average age of immigrants with a party affiliation is 40, and their average length of time in the United States is 17 years, compared to 37 years of age and 12 years of residency for immigrants without an affiliation. The political efficacy scores for foreign-born Hispanics who were interviewed in English is 3.6, compared to 3.0 for foreign-born respondents who were interviewed in Spanish. These findings tell us that although as a group immigrants may express relatively low levels of political efficacy, it is important that subgroups within the immigrant population be taken into consideration to gain a more complete picture of how they feel about being politically empowered.

Conclusion

Attitudes can serve as a basis for cooperation and consensus. When different groups such as Hispanics and African Americans share similar views, disagreements are held to a minimum and mutual respect, understanding, and cooperation become possible. Cooperation is especially important for Hispanics and African Americans because both groups are in a subordinate status, face common obstacles, and comprise the majority of the population in Houston. If they are able to build on their commonalities, a long-lasting coalition is possible and mutual efforts to improve their status are strengthened.

The areas in which agreement exists are support for prayer in the public schools, protection of gay rights, the importance of the family, government support for the needy, preserving ethnic identity and culture, and support of a national identification card. Both groups believe that discrimination can be overcome and that Hispanics do not have too much power and are not prejudiced against African Americans and that Hispanics are not members of the White race. Their relationship was defined as good by a majority of both groups, and the issues that both feel they should work on are getting along, obtaining a better education, and combating discrimination. While the intensity of such views was not assessed, it is reasonable to assume, given each group's history, that both feel strongly about the need for education, challenging discrimination, and receiving the support of government. Also, recall from chapter 2 that both groups describe each other with many of the same terms (e.g., friendly, nice, good people, considerate, fair). Again, these common perceptions serve as a basis for cooperation and coalition building.

A promising area for coalition is electoral politics. Together, Hispanics and African Americans account for approximately 40 percent of the total votes cast in citywide elections. Both tend to vote for Democrats and support the same political agenda, such as affirmative action and a larger role for government in ensuring fairness. If they unite and vote as a bloc they can strongly influence if not dictate the winner of any citywide election. However, given the relative disparity in their voting strength, a political coalition may involve African Americans in the leadership role, at least for the immediate future.

U.S.-born Hispanics and African Americans seem destined to play a special role in fostering goodwill between their communities. On the one hand, U.S.-born Hispanics have more interaction with African Americans, are more sympathetic to their issues, have more knowledge of their history, and view them more favorably in comparison to foreign-born Hispanics. U.S.-born Hispanics and African Americans also share and have more knowledge of American culture. On the other hand, many U.S.-born Hispanics are the sons and daughters of Hispanic immigrants and thus have a familial bond with foreign-born Hispanics. Also, U.S.-born Hispanics are closer to foreign-born Hispanics socially, culturally, and in physical appearance. Thus they are "in between" both groups and are in a position to promote better understanding and better relations between African American and foreign-born Hispanics, especially in work sites and other community settings where all three groups are present.

African Americans can also play a crucial role in promoting cooperation because they perceive Hispanics more favorably than they are perceived by Hispanics and because they are more willing to date and marry Hispanics than vice versa. This greater acceptance means that African Americans, like U.S.-born Hispanics, may have to take the leadership role in fostering good relations. Within each group those who have the more favorable views of each other and who understand the power of coalition will have to take the lead.

Chapter 6

Prospects for Black-Brown Relations

What it's going to take basically is some educated people to take some people who are not so stereotypical or have so many bad perceptions of each culture. You have to get people in there [politics] who actually want to work together, but I think it will work. It's going to take some people who have a similar vision and people who are willing to sit down and talk, which is not happening right now. Everybody's out for their own stuff right now.

THIRTY-FIVE-YEAR-OLD BLACK FEMALE

The 2000 U.S. Census showed that the projected population growth of Hispanics to a number greater than that of African Americans had already occurred in Houston. This demographic development raises a host of Black-Brown issues, of course, many of which we examined in the previous chapters. But before we review our findings, it may be helpful to briefly list some of the developments in Black-Brown relations around the country in the past year.

- In Los Angeles, California, a popular Hispanic narrowly loses the opportunity to become the city's first Hispanic mayor after his White opponent receives strong African American voter support.

- In Georgia, Black state legislators at first resist the idea of defining Hispanics in the state as "minorities" but later change their minds after meeting with national Hispanic leaders.

- In Paterson, New Jersey, Hispanics accuse an African American youth of a hate crime after a group of Black teenagers beat a Hispanic homeless man to death following a fight between African American and Hispanic youths at a local high school.

- In Austin, Texas, African American state legislators help to pass a bill, signed into law, that opens up state colleges and universities to undocumented immigrant students, mainly Hispanics, who have lived in the state for a number of years.

As these cases illustrate, there is no clear-cut pattern of Black-Brown relations. Every setting seems to bring a different set of opportunities for conflict and cooperation. But what is clear is that this relational sphere will remain very dynamic if for no other reason than that the Hispanic population remains in a state of steady growth supported by high levels of immigration. Indeed, the Mexican government's strong support for an open border policy with the United States could make this source of Hispanic population growth a permanent feature. African American leaders have often supported Hispanic immigration, but it is logical to question if this will continue when Hispanics begin to greatly outpace Blacks in historically Black domains in communities across the country, such as in the rural labor markets of the Deep South. Black-Brown solidarity in the civil rights movement of the 1950s and 1960s made sense when both groups were struggling against a common history of racial oppression, but will it mean the same in the twenty-first century when the social histories of the new Hispanics are grounded in other national experiences? Or will the continuing history of racial and ethnic inequality in the United States (Feagin, Vera, and Batur 2001) continue to promote alliances among groups at the lowest rungs of the country's social ladder?

It may not be an exaggeration to characterize the beginning of the twenty-first century in Houston as a period in which African Americans arrived politically; perhaps it can even be called the golden age of African American political power. An African American mayor, an African American police chief, an African American superintendent, an African American member of Congress, an African American head of Metro, significantly more African American than Hispanic city departmental officials—all indicate that African Americans have reached an unprecedented level of political power in the city. Given this political ascendance, it was perhaps fitting that in 2000 the former Woolworth building at the corner of Main and Elgin Streets near downtown was torn down to make way for a parking garage. The building was a vestige of Jim Crowism when Blacks were not allowed to sit at the food counter of the Woolworth store. It was the first segregated eating area targeted by Black protestors at the beginning of the civil rights movement in Houston.

Hispanics have also had a significant measure of political ascendancy in the Houston area at the beginning of the twenty-first century but with less visible success. Moreover, the political ascendancy of Hispanics has not been directly proportional to their population growth. Although Hispanics outnumber African Americans in the city by more than two hundred thousand, the Houston area has more Black elected officials than Hispanic elected officials, twenty-four to eighteen, respectively. To some extent, Hispanic political development in the city has been characterized by moments of internal division. To be sure, all groups experience internal political divisions that can weaken their political unity. For example, at times some Black politicians take conservative stances or side with conservative Whites, which puts them at odds with the liberal views of many established Black leaders in the city. Among Hispanics the divisions have involved such developments as the fragmentation of the old Mexican American political networks, the arrival of non-Mexican-origin Hispanic political leaders, the growth of multinational and transnational political issues, and the emergence of a political leadership type that separates ethnic identity from ethnic concerns. Internal Hispanic political divisions do not necessarily mean that Hispanics engage in constant political infighting. What these divisions mean is that Hispanic political unity cannot be assumed and that this unity remains an empirical question, especially for Hispanic leaders.

Large-scale immigration is a major factor driving Hispanic segmentation in Houston. Although immigration has increased the Hispanic population to a level that exceeds that of African Americans, it has also created challenges to Hispanic unity across the city. Some immigrants are still in an early stage of adaptation in which they feel little social and cultural identity with the longer-established Hispanics, especially the Mexican American population (Bach 1993). Indeed, some Hispanic newcomers complain that Mexican Americans discriminate against them (Niemann et al. 1999). On the other hand, some U.S.-born Hispanics see new Hispanic immigrants as job competitors (Rodriguez 1995). For many Hispanic immigrants, the major political concerns are federal immigration policies and developments back home, not local ethnic politics. The heightened diversity of Hispanic immigrants in the city, including diversity within the different national-origin groups (e.g., the Maya and non-Maya from Guatemala and Garifuna and other Hispanics from Honduras), makes it almost impossible to categorize all Latin American immigrants in the city as Hispanic. In everyday life, the more realistic social and cultural situation is that there is not one but several Hispanic populations in the city.

The effects of intra-Hispanic segmentation should not be overstated, however. While various Hispanic groups in Houston may remain socially and culturally distant, as our survey shows, they often come together attitudinally and at least symbolically share major group orientations.

Finally, immigration is significantly affecting the level of political capital among Hispanics, especially compared to African Americans. Among Hispanic immigrants in our survey only about 20 percent reported being U.S. citizens. Given that immigrants represent about 55 percent of all Hispanic adults in the city, this low naturalization rate means that only 56 percent of Hispanic adults are eligible to vote in elections. By contrast, among African Americans, 97 percent of whom were born in the United States, voter eligibility approaches 100 percent. The point is clear in comparing the political capital of Hispanics and African Americans in Houston: Hispanics have the largest racial-ethnic population, but African Americans have the largest racial-ethnic voter population. It will take some years before Hispanics can reduce the political gap with African Americans.

Accommodation or Conflict?

There are no clear signs at the turn of the twenty-first century that Black-Brown relations in Houston, or in the rest of the country, are unequivocally headed for either accommodation or conflict. Looking at Black-Brown relations in Houston in the past few years, one can expect that in the near term these relations will continue to be characterized mainly by accommodation but with occasional tension and conflict. Public schools are a key setting of conflict, perhaps because they are among the first institutions to be affected by a wide range of age cohorts from new populations (in comparison to nursing homes, for example, which are affected only by the elderly population). A few cases help to illustrate how schools are sometimes the setting for tense Black-Brown relations. Some Blacks watch with concern as Hispanic enrollment increases sharply in some of the school district's historically Black high schools. Jones and Wheatly High Schools, for example, were overwhelmingly Black as recently as the late 1980s, but by the 1999–2000 school year Black student enrollment had dropped sharply to 51 percent and 52 percent, respectively, while Hispanic enrollment had increased to 41 percent and 47 percent, respectively

(Houston Independent School District 1988, 2000). Black alumni of historically Black high schools sometimes see the increase in Hispanic enrollment as a threat to what have been core educational institutions in the development of the city's African American community. Some Hispanics, on the other hand, question why less than 20 percent of the school district's teaching and counseling staff is Hispanic but more than 40 percent Black when Hispanic students account for a majority of the district's enrollment (the school district has an active program to recruit bilingual teachers in Latin America and other regions of the world).

In a heated and emotional issue for many Hispanics in the city, in summer 1999 the African American members of the Houston Independent School Board voted with other board members, but against two long-term Hispanic members, to fast-track Hispanic students out of the school system's bilingual education program. Though the new bilingual education policy was cosponsored by a Mexican American board member, a newcomer to Houston's political scene, a long list of established Hispanic leaders vigorously opposed it. To be sure, the Hispanic leaders who opposed the new policy did not view the African American board members as political adversaries; rather, the Hispanic leaders' view was that the school board was insensitive to the cultural concerns of the Hispanic population.

Although school issues can cause tension and conflict between African Americans and Hispanics, other issues can help to bring about accommodation. For example, U.S. representative Sheila Jackson Lee supported federal policies to assist immigrants. A significant number of the city's almost three hundred thousand Latin American immigrants are undocumented or have been granted some form of temporary protective status by the federal government. Jackson Lee, an African American woman and the Houston area's only racial minority member of Congress, represents a congressional district that is over one-fourth Hispanic. Jackson Lee has steadfastly and enthusiastically supported policy proposals in Congress that if adopted into law would alleviate the legal, residential problems of many Hispanic immigrants in Houston and across the country. While many other Democratic U.S. representatives also support such measures, Jackson Lee does so in Houston, which has the largest African American population of any southern city, and in which, as our survey shows, a large proportion of this population has negative attitudes toward immigrants.

At the beginning of the twenty-first century, in the everyday life of

Houston the pattern of Black-Brown relations appears to be multilevel and developing around specific situations. The issues that affect relations between African American and Hispanic leaders in the political sphere seem to be greatly removed from those that affect residents in local neighborhood settings, especially in the city's large inner-city working-class areas. For example, in the inner-city Third Ward, which is one of the original African American settlements in Houston, the new presence of Hispanic immigrant residents seems to raise mainly the issue of parking space availability. The new Hispanic residents, drawn by the lower rents in the neighborhood, pursue normal family lives but remain linguistically separate from their African American neighbors. In a public housing project in the neighborhood, African Americans and Hispanics also reside in apparent harmony but without much visible interaction. The occasional scene of mixed African American and Hispanic children play groups indicates that intergroup accommodation is not totally passive in the neighborhood. In the Bottoms, a lower-working-class section of the neighborhood, one gets the impression that both African American and Hispanic residents are more concerned with scratching out a living than with their group leaders' conduct in ethnic politics.

Implications of the Survey Findings

The many findings of our survey study have important implications for the prospect of Black-Brown relations in Houston. In this section we review the salient general findings and discuss what they suggest for the future, as well as their implications for improving relations between the two groups.

In chapter 2 we saw that *both* African Americans and Hispanics hold a long list of stereotypes about each other. This is not a surprising finding, given the maintenance of consensual, societal stereotypes. Intergroup stereotypes are also a common condition in many multigroup settings (e.g., Winborne and Cohen 1998). We found that in general African Americans think more positively about Hispanics than do Hispanics about African Americans. Moreover, some African Americans offered stereotypes that portrayed Hispanics as economic competitors.

It is safe to assume that some of the negative stereotypical beliefs that Hispanics have about African Americans are not the result of the specific setting of Houston but of historical and almost universal racism (Feagin 1988) that can be traced back at least to the subjugation of Black people in the era of European colonialism during the formation of the capitalist world system (Green 1997). The implication is that for local settings to have a better chance of reducing negative stereotypes, racist imaging must be reduced at the macrostructural level, for example, the international entertainment media. The perception of primarily lower-income African Americans that Hispanics are economic competitors is not surprising, given that for the most economically subordinated in the labor market, the increasing presence of other workers, especially immigrant ones, can only be seen as an economic threat. The reduction of negative stereotypes among this economically disadvantaged population must come mainly from their own social mobility, given the permanent presence of immigrant labor in the U.S. labor market. Upward social mobility is dependent on a strong and growing labor market, which has been the case in Houston since the early 1900s. Yet historically labor markets have been segmented, offering fewer opportunities for mobility to workers with low human capital.

While U.S.-born Hispanics expressed more positive views of African Americans than did foreign-born Hispanics, the two groups agreed closely in their lists of stereotypes. However, meanings attached to listed traits differed significantly between U.S.-born and foreign-born Hispanics in the extent to which terms were considered positive, with the latter group considering the terms more negative. This finding indicates that we cannot pay attention simply to the content of stereotypes. Rather, to understand relations between groups, we must also understand how different ethnic groups interpret the behaviors and traits embedded in stereotypes.

Another major finding is that Hispanics who expressed pride in their ethnic group tended strongly to rate African Americans positively. The implication of this finding for promoting positive intergroup relations is obvious: all efforts to promote Hispanic ethnic pride also have the benefit of tending to increase Hispanic positive attitudes toward African Americans. This is a major practical implication because it suggests remedial action can be undertaken locally without waiting for universal macrostructural change to occur.

Chapter 3 focused on the specific arenas of social life where African Americans and Hispanics diverged, that is, where the two groups expressed disagreements or desires for separation or expressed sentiments of conflict. Both groups gave their lowest approval to the statement about their children dating or marrying someone from the other group. To be sure, African Americans were more approving of dating and marrying Hispanics than Hispanics were of dating and marrying African Americans. The preference for keeping dating and marriage within the group no doubt is affected by the maintenance of ethnic-racial boundaries, which reflects U.S. societal norms. That is, in contrast to the relative ethnic amorphousness of the White population, many African Americans and Hispanics have strong and clear subcultural group identities supported by a variety of traits, such as language. In the subcultural world there is a strong and clear sense of who are members of the group and who are not.

The Hispanic belief that government programs favor African Americans and that African Americans have too much power is probably related to the more general view held by many Hispanics that African Americans are considered the country's first racial minority group and that Hispanics occupy second place. The greater visibility of African Americans in government office tends to promote this view. It is likely that the Hispanic perception of governmental favoritism of Blacks will diminish only when government programs are curtailed for everyone or when Hispanics have greater visibility at various governmental levels. As indicated earlier, in Houston Hispanics benefit more from affirmative action than do African Americans and White women.

African Americans' negative assessment of immigrants' impact in the Houston area, described in chapter 3, may not be attributable only to concerns over economic competition. Other factors may be at play among a majority—but not a large majority—of African Americans who hold this view. No doubt many African Americans, like other Americans, were affected by the anti-immigrant statements of various leaders in the 1990s, statements that endorsed such restrictive measures as Proposition 187 in California and the 1996 U.S. Immigration Act. The finding that more than 40 percent of African Americans also gave negative views of the use of the Spanish language in the United States suggests that the recentness and rapid rate of immigration may be a factor relevant to this assessment. Although Hispanics and the Spanish language have been part of the Houston scene since the 1800s, it has only been in the last two and a half decades that Hispanics and Spanish have spread to almost all the sectors of the city of Houston. Before the mid-1970s the larger numbers of Hispanics (Mexican Americans) resided in the eastern half of the city, and Spanish, when it was heard publicly, was limited to a couple of radio stations. Today Hispanics and their cultural representations are omnipresent in the city, including Spanish-language radio and television programs. A Spanish-language radio station that caters primarily to Mexican immigrants is the most popular station in the city. If the recentness of and unfamiliarity with the Spanish language is a factor affecting the negative perceptions of African Americans, then this negativity can be expected to decline as African Americans become more accustomed to their increasingly Hispanicized social environment. However, if a future political mobilization of Hispanics in the city involves the symbolic use of Spanish to muster Hispanic solidarity, then we can expect that African Americans will view Spanish not as a neutral trait of their multicultural environment but as a political weapon that can be used against them.

The finding reported in chapter 3 that African American women tend to see immigrants as economic competitors and believe that Hispanics look down on Blacks suggests that any efforts to improve relations between the two populations should especially take the views of these women into account. Actually, the same applies for Hispanic women, as it was older Hispanic females who expressed the least approval of Black-Brown dating and intermarriage.

Chapter 4, which examined women's responses to our survey in detail, showed the higher sense of Black-Brown divergence and conflict expressed by women of both groups. The generality of this gender differentiation makes the findings worth repeating. First, among both U.S.- and foreign-born Hispanics, the women were more likely than their male counterparts to express feelings of competition or conflict between African Americans and Hispanics. Second, among U.S.- and foreign-born Hispanic women, the foreign born were more likely to express feelings of competition or conflict between the two groups. Finally, among African Americans, the women were more likely than the men to express feelings of competition and conflict between the two groups.

These findings strongly reinforce the suggestion that efforts to reduce negative intergroup perceptions must especially take into account the involvement of women. The concern is more than just that women tend to score higher on scales of intergroup division but, as explained in chapter 4, that women in both groups play a special role in the nurturing of children. Given this role, it is logical that negative intergroup perceptions among the women can be passed on to their children. Of course, significant variations in the women's perceptions occur across different levels of contact, social class, and culture.

We must remember that the quantity and quality of intergroup interaction is also a function of societal racism. What is important for the formation of different intergroup perceptions is the nature of intergroup contact. The results of focus group meetings with Hispanic women indicated that some of these women formed negative views of African Americans based on their encounters with African American women in public service settings. These Black-Brown encounters, which are a frequent daily occurrence in Houston's public service institutions, are by their nature some of the most detrimental to promoting positive intergroup perceptions and relations. The encounters involve immigrants who are often desperately in need of assistance from agencies they see as bureaucratically and culturally cold and distant if not hostile. From the perspective of the African American service providers in the public agencies, the encounters involve dealing with foreigners who have difficulty speaking English and who frequently are not even legally in the country. Frustration and suspicion are pitted against each other. No positive relations can be expected to result from these encounters. The solutions to reducing the negativity that results from dysfunctional encounters such as these for both Hispanics and African Americans must involve social and cultural acclimation to the greater Hispanic immigrant presence and greater employment of bilingual personnel in public service agencies.

A series of findings presented in chapter 5 indicated how African Americans and Hispanics in Houston share similar attitudes on a variety of issues. Specifically, African Americans and Hispanics agreed on supporting such issues as allowing prayer in public schools, providing government assistance to the disadvantaged, supporting gay rights, recognizing the primacy of the family, maintaining an ethnic identity, and using a national identification card to keep undocumented workers from U.S. jobs. African Americans and Hispanics also expressed consensus on several issues regarding relations between their two groups. A majority in both groups feel that the effects of discrimination can be overcome, that African Americans do not fear Hispanics, that Hispanics are not prejudiced against Blacks, that Hispanics do not have too much power, that Black-Brown relations are somewhat or very good, and that Hispanics are not members of the White race. All these findings are encouraging from the standpoint of a common base from which to promote positive relations between the two groups, but the perception that Hispanics are not White may be particularly significant, as it implies the absence of a racial divide between the two groups. Yet almost one-fourth of U.S.-born Hispanics and more than one-third of foreign-born Hispanics agreed with the survey statement that Hispanics are members of the White race. Given the diversity of national origins among Hispanics, it is likely that some Hispanic groups may have a greater White racial identity than others. For some Hispanics, this identification with the White race may be a function of the stigma associated with people of color in the United States. Some Hispanic groups (e.g., Cubans) have experienced more stratified race relations with Blacks than other Hispanic groups (e.g., Mexicans).

We found that Hispanics fear African Americans. This fear is likely the result of negative stereotypes about African American men in particular. This stereotype can be diffused with quality, equal-status contact between the groups. A key point to consider, however, is that not all Hispanics may share the same interest in enhancing positive relations between African Americans and Hispanics.

That both African Americans and Hispanics reported "working together on getting along" as one of their top three projects for mutual cooperation indicates a predisposition to improve relations between the two groups. This predisposition can serve as a key resource for organizing activities to accomplish this. Moreover, this finding indicates that it should not be a major task—if it is a task at all—to convince African Americans and Hispanics on the usefulness of these types of activities. The ideological work appears already to have been accomplished.

Forming Closer Intergroup Relations through a Common Group Identity

How might a common group identity be formed for African Americans and Hispanics? The answer to this question lies in the reasons that a common identity works to enhance group relations. Although stereotypes affect perceptions and relations, leaders may reduce intergroup hostility and enhance overall group relations by effecting a positive shift in stereotypes. This shift may be precipitated by a focus on a common group identity, based on common group predicaments, common goals, and common values. The research on stereotypes we have presented indicates that the time is right for ethnic-racial group leaders to focus on these common issues. This focus on commonality will not only enhance group relations, it will increase the chances that, working together, African Americans and Hispanics will accomplish their shared goals of enhanced quality of life, including improved health care and access to education and diminished ethnic-racial oppression and discrimination.

African American and Hispanic group leaders must focus on the common predicament of subordination and alleviation of the substandard quality of life relative to Whites in the United States. Examples of issues that need to be addressed are health, education, career opportunities, political representation, and wage parity with Whites. This focus may shift the competition between African and Hispanics and the sense of social displacement to competition with the dominant group, which controls resources. Focusing on common goals also serves to focus on values, which are considered more important than traits (Schwartz and Struch 1989). "Beliefs about a groups' hierarchy of basic values reflect the way a person perceives the humanity of the members of that group" (Schwartz and Struch 1989, 164).

Leaders can focus on common values relative to equal opportunity and diminished discrimination in the United States for both African Americans and persons of Mexican descent. This focus is likely to positively affect intergroup stereotypes. Stereotypes function as theoretical naive explanations of the world; they are not necessarily rigid but can be flexible (Leyens, Yzerbyt, and Schadron 1994). Stereotypes change as reality changes, and therefore they can be changed by focusing on a common identity (Oakes, Haslam, and Turner 1994). As stereotypes become more positive, intergroup relations will likely become more positive.

A new group identity can be created that merges two independent groups simply by giving the two groups a common label, such as "people of color." This identity is not expected to replace the existing ethnic-racial group identity but simply add a new social identity for all group members. "Indeed, in some respects, a simultaneous recognition of both group difference and group commonality may be particularly valuable and beneficial" (Dovidio, Gaertner, and Validzic 1998, 117).

The common identity model works because it affects emotion toward a group (Dovidio, Gaertner, and Validzic 1998). Negative emotions are diffused when the focus is on commonalities. Common group identity facilitates thinking of each other as equals. Equal relative status, rather than absolute status, is key to successful contact. We must recognize the importance of social categorization for promoting positive bias and creating conditions for successful contact, in part by transforming members' cognitive representation of the membership from separate groups to one, more inclusive group (Gaertner et al. 1995). Indeed, research indicates that more inclusive one-group representation critically mediates the relationship between conditions of intergroup contact and the reduction of bias (Dovidio, Gaertner, and Validzic 1998).

Prospects for Common Group Unity

In this section, we look at the prospects for common group unity between African Americans and Hispanics in Houston from the perspectives of intermarriage, a common Houstonian identity, a common social class status, and a common history of minority group status.

Effects of Intermarriage

According to census statistics, the intermarriage rate among African Africans in the United States increased from 6 percent in 1980 to 9 percent in 1997 (U.S. Census Bureau 1998, table 67). Among Hispanics, the rate declined from 32 percent in 1980 to 29 percent in 1997. Both measures are good indicators that intermarriage can be one process that promotes common group unity between African Americans and Hispanics. Although the intermarriage rate of African Americans has increased only slightly, it has increased. As we showed in chapter 3, large proportions of African Americans and U.S.- and foreign-born Hispanics indicated that it was all right for their children to marry a member of the other group. Among African Americans, greater approval was given by the younger respondents, especially males. Some African American women in the Houston area have a preference for Hispanic men over non-Hispanic White men in considerations of intermarriage, although some African American women were concerned that Hispanic women compete with them for African American men and that African American men sometimes show a preference for Hispanic women. (It is possible that the reverse can happen, that is, that Hispanic women become concerned if they perceive that African American women are paying an inordinate amount of attention to Hispanic men.)

The reason we consider the decrease in the Hispanic intermarriage rate a good indicator of future prospects for more Hispanic intermarriage is that it is occurring in the context of the largest wave of Hispanic immigration in the country's history. In the past two decades, immigration has accounted for approximately half of the Hispanic population growth in the United States. A decrease of only 3 percent in Hispanic intermarriage in this context means that Hispanic intermarriage is still substantial and probably still increasing significantly in absolute numbers. Many Hispanic immigrants arrive in the country already married (to other Hispanics), and many new Hispanic immigrants who are not yet socially assimilated tend mainly to marry other Hispanics. Given that propinquity plays a key part in the selection of a marital partner, it is likely that Black-Brown intermarriage will increase in Houston, where since the 1980s younger members of the two groups have increasingly shared social spaces (e.g., high schools, universities, and the new mixed neighborhoods of the city's far southwest side). Yet there is no reason to expect that an increase in Black-Brown intermarriage would be more than low to moderate, meaning that intermarriage by itself cannot play a leading role in promoting positive relations between the two groups.

Common Houstonian Identity

Houston, like other dynamic urban settings, has undertaken organized efforts to foster a sense of common identity and pride among the city's residents. For example, after an economic downturn caused the Houston area's economy to lose some two hundred thousand jobs in the early 1980s, the city's business sector created a Houston Proud movement (Feagin 1988). Many businesses in the city answered their telephones with the slogan "Houston Proud" and in other ways used the slogan in promotion campaigns. Houston boosterism campaigns are serious operations led by prominent executives from major companies and banks (Feagin 1988). The city's professional sports team can also inspire a strong sense of common identity and pride when they have successful seasons. When the Rockets and the Comets won national basketball championships in the 1990s many residents felt they were Houstonians first and members of specific ethnic or racial groups second. In basketball arenas, baseball parks, and football stadiums, Black and Brown Houston fans can quickly find a common cause. The question remains, however, if the moments of intergroup solidarity in these sports settings can carry over into the larger community.

In the absence of data, it is not unreasonable to suggest that persons who frequently attend sports events alongside other ethnic and racial group members may be more accepting of intergroup relations than persons who do not have close intergroup encounters with a similar common purpose. The solidarity that forms in boosterism campaigns or during recreational activities may not itself create common group unity in the larger community, but it certainly provides a familiarity if not an identity with the other that can make further intergroup exchanges easier. Of course, the way recreational events are organized can affect the prospects for intergroup relations. The Houston Livestock and Rodeo Show draws the largest paying crowd of all recreational activities in Houston, but the event probably has a lower payoff for promoting intergroup relations, as the evening music entertainment program caters to particular groups (e.g., Hispanics and country-western fans) on separate nights. Moreover, the decision of the event's board in the mid-1990s to disqualify nonciti-zen students from the college scholarship program it operates with the event's revenues created a cleavage among some Hispanic residents.

In the United States, sports have historically played a crucial role in the general recognition and acknowledgment of the skills and compe-tencies of members of different ethnic-racial groups. Like intermarriage, however, professional sports events that promote a common Housto-nian identity cannot by themselves be the major source for positive Black-Brown relations in the city. At baseball games, for example, African Americans and Hispanics usually make up only a small percentage of the fans present, though the two groups comprise a greater share of the tele-vision audience. Yet sports events collectively, as well as other settings (religious, work, etc.) that have an African American and Hispanic pres-ence, help to form the social infrastructure and the wider social environ-ment within which the dynamics of Black-Brown relations evolve. That several leading baseball players in the United States are Black Hispanics only helps to promote the significance of sports for positive Black-Brown relations. No single component of this setting has determinant power, but together the components constitute the contextual forces that move Black-Brown relations forward.

Shared Social Class Status

The 1990 census showed that the largest numbers of African Americans and Hispanics in Houston overlapped considerably in occupational dis-tribution (U.S. Census Bureau 1993, tables 23 and 29). Except for a higher social class segment of the city that extends southwesterly into Fort Bend County, the majority of African American and Hispanic workers in the central city in Harris County have blue-collar or lower-skill white-collar jobs. In other words, many African Americans and Hispanics in the cen-tral city have a common lower-middle-class or working-class status, at lower income levels; the 1990 census found a median family income of about $20,000 per year for both groups in the central city in Harris

County. The occupational overlap of African Americans and Hispanics is a major reason that both groups reported in our survey that the work site is the primary place of frequent interaction with members of the other group.

In a variety of survey questions, African Americans and Hispanics answered with one voice regarding the need for more government assistance programs, yet this unity does not seem to emanate from a common occupational or social class identity. Frequently, African American and Hispanic workers are found in segregated work crews or are divided by tasks in the companies where they work. This situation is in part a natural outgrowth of the ethnic and racial composition of the city's labor market, but it is also a deliberate strategy of employers to capitalize on the cheaper and more tractable Hispanic immigrant labor. After a while employers may turn completely to Hispanic immigrants to fill their labor bill, creating major divisions between African American and Hispanic workers in the same industries and occupations.

African Americans and Hispanics are aware that they substantially share the same social class status, yet this has not developed into a city-wide common intergroup unity. To be sure, in U.S. social history, class usually has not been a major unifying force among culturally different groups. That is to say, it has not developed into a "class-for-itself" condition predicted by theorists of industrial society (e.g., Dahrendorf 1959). Yet the absence of this development does not mean that a common social class status is useless for promoting greater solidarity between African Americans and Hispanics. At the very least, a common social class status serves as a major potential resource for greater Black-Brown unity. As we discuss in the section below, the crucial variable is what use African American and Hispanic leaders make of this potential.

Similar Minority Group Experience

The recognition of their common experience as members of oppressed groups in the United States may hold substantial potential for unity of African Americans and Hispanics. There is no question that African Americans generally experienced much harsher prejudice and discrimination than Hispanics in U.S. history. However, apart from the extreme cruelties of slavery and Jim Crowism, especially in the pre–World War II years, both groups have had a similar minority group experience of exclusion and marginalization in the United States. Both groups have suffered educational segregation, economic subordination, and political oppression because of their identifiable group characteristics. While members of both groups are now found in high administrative positions and elected offices, African Americans and Hispanics are still markedly absent from the boards of major U.S. corporations and banks, not to mention from the most prestigious social circles in the country. In many significant ways, African Americans and Hispanics, including those at higher income levels, remain minority populations excluded from full participation in the institutions of U.S. society. Given this common experience, it is plausible to expect that the two groups will be motivated to form a collective power through solidarity and unity. Indeed, this happens frequently in many settings across Houston. In workplaces, community meetings, and professional coalitions, African Americans and Hispanics often express values and desires for mutual support and collaboration. Sometimes this is an unspoken understanding, especially in the presence of Whites with superior power or authority. The question remains, however, why this desire for a mutually beneficial collaboration has not generated a greater degree of common identity and unity than presently exists between the two groups.

One reason is that cases of Black-Brown collaboration based on a common purpose tend to be ad hoc and temporary. For example, African American and Hispanic political leaders or health care professionals may unite on a specific political race or health care issue, but the unity ends when the goal becomes attainable or is reached. It is unrealistic to expect that Black-Brown unity in one sector (e.g., politics or health care) will automatically extend into other sectors, as different sectors usually have different sets of actors and agendas. Another reason that instances of Black-Brown collaboration do not develop into sustained efforts is that third parties can create divisions between African Americans and Hispanics. For example, African American and Hispanic health professionals may come together to organize a community blood drive, but if public health agencies offer special grant support to either the African American or the Hispanic community, then the health professionals from the favored group may lose interest in an intergroup coalition. This example illustrates that larger, institutional, contextual factors can influence significantly the intergroup decision making of African Americans and Hispanics.

Perhaps the most important reason that collaboration between African Americans and Hispanics has not generated a greater degree of common identity and unity is their different experiences as subcultures. Both groups have survived under conditions of social subordination mainly by mustering internal community strength. Both groups survived because they strengthened their internal cultural institutions, not because they weakened their intergroup boundaries. In the absence of external sources of support in the pre–civil rights period, internal fortification became a crucial mode of survival. Intergroup collaboration may make good political logic, but it makes poor cultural logic. From this subcultural perspective, a sustained Black-Brown common identity and unity will develop when both groups become more assimilated into the mainstream and thus become more similar culturally.

Finally, Hispanic and African American leaders have not generally promoted unity. The attitudes and behaviors of group leaders are crucial to present and future intergroup relations. Below we discuss the role of different types of African American and Hispanic elected and community-based leaders in promoting intergroup collaboration.

Implications for Community Leaders

Apart from subcultural differences, the fact remains that in the everyday life of Houston, African Americans and Hispanics stand to gain much by losing their prejudices and developing greater unity. Promoting Black-Brown harmony and cooperation, rather than conflict and division, makes particular sense at the beginning of the twenty-first century when together African Americans and Hispanics constitute almost two-thirds of Houston's population. In several ways African Americans and Hispanics in Houston have great potential for a higher level of common unity. Leaders in both groups can and must play an important role for this potential to be realized, especially in terms of common social issues. To assess the feasibility of this leadership, it is useful to briefly review the types of African American and Hispanic leadership that currently operate in the Houston scene. We distinguish four types.

The first type is the leader involved in traditional ethnic politics. Ideologically, these individuals are concerned primarily with promoting the interests of their own group. They are identified publicly or privately as ethnic group leaders and receive the support of their followers primarily because of this identity. Most of the pioneer and many of the present African American and Hispanic leaders in the city traveled this road to power. They fought for their groups' interests in city hall, in courts, in school board offices, in backrooms, and on the streets. These leaders may appear outdated in an approaching post–affirmative action era, which will supposedly promote a color-blind society, but it was mainly their efforts that brought their groups needed resources and political empowerment. It is this self-interest, however, that limits the traditional ethnic political leaders from becoming the strongest promoters of African American and Hispanic unity. They can and have played a constructive role in furthering unity between the two groups, because they share common minority goals, for example, redistricting to create more representatives for both communities and supporting affirmative action policies, but their own-group orientation limits their capacity to think in terms of a common identity.

The second type of ethnic leadership consists of those who benefit from their ethnic identity, recognized by themselves or by others, but who do little or nothing on behalf of their ethnic group. These individuals can be greatly valued by Whites because their presence enables Whites to support an ethnic-identified leader who likely will not work against their interests and indeed may even promote them to garner White support. New ethnic leaders have low capacity for promoting unity between African Americans and Hispanics because they do not usually function ideologically along ethnic-defined lines. Moreover, ethnic group members may hold them in suspicion for their lack of ethnic allegiance. Between the traditional ethnic group leader and the new ethnic leader, it is the former who can do more to promote African American–Hispanic unity because it is the former who has more grassroots support and connections.

The third type is ethnic group members who have reached prominent, institutional positions working on behalf of power interests outside the African American or Hispanic communities, whether visibly or invisibly. Although they do not espouse an ethnic ideology, they nonetheless usually achieve considerable distinction in the community because they have reached high positions, especially for ethnic group members, and they have the support of both their ethnic group and the larger power interests. These leaders have a key function in the political age of diversification: they enable power elites to continue operating even when the political scene becomes substantially diversified. These ethnic leaders can play a useful role in promoting unity between African Americans and Hispanics because they have a respectable identity in the community, and they have access to larger mainstream resources through their ties to dominant interests. But they can promote intergroup unity only if it meets the approval of the dominant interests (usually White) that they are aligned with.

The fourth type of African American and Hispanic ethnic leader is one who promotes and practices an ideology of intergroup collaboration and unity. This is a dynamic leadership group, although still very much in the minority, and some of its members are constantly involved in a host of forums, seminars, workshops, and conferences that address issues of intergroup relations. Some members of this ethnic leadership type developed their intergroup interests through personal experiences and others through corporate or community training programs on leadership in a culturally diversifying society. Needless to say, this type of ethnic leader can serve as a valuable resource for building greater unity between African Americans and Hispanics. Indeed, at the middle-class and corporate levels where many of these community leaders are found, they have already done much to start breaking down stereotypical and relational barriers among groups.

Yet even this type of ethnic leader is limited to some extent in the ability to create greater intergroup unity. One limitation is that at present this community leadership is contained mainly in middle-class domains of more educated and higher-income members and thus appears unable to extend its coalition building to working-class African Americans and Hispanics in the inner city. In addition, this type of ethnic leader has become so immersed in the ideal of intergroup collaboration that he or she will sometimes refuse to participate in a collaborative effort that does not include all the major ethnic-racial groups in the city.

This brief review reveals another layer of the complex factors affecting relations between African Americans and Hispanics in Houston. Yet a key point remains: as previous research has indicated, striving for common group identity and unity reduces prejudices and divisions, and community leaders have a major role to play in this process. Regardless of the type of leadership, the more African American and Hispanic leaders impress on their followers that the two groups have common interests, the greater the chances that the two groups can establish unity in the Houston area. This leadership task is of the highest priority. We believe that it is not an overstatement to say that time may be running out.

Already the Hispanic population in Houston has grown significantly larger than the African American population, and this disparity will surely deepen as large-scale immigration continues to drive Hispanic population growth. Eventually, this demographic force will narrow the

Hispanic political gap with Blacks, as more Hispanic immigrants become naturalized citizens and their U.S.-born children reach voting age (which is already occurring). There is no guarantee of positive political outcomes when Hispanics reach political equity with African Americans in the city. Indeed, the mayoral runoff election between Brown and Sanchez indicated that Hispanics can mobilize into an ethnic voting bloc as easily as Blacks—and against a Black candidate. In Houston, African Americans and Hispanics still have a choice in the intergroup direction they want to take, and community leaders from both groups have an important role to play in this decision.

Future Research

Many research questions remain outside the scope of our data and outside the findings of the limited number of studies on Black-Brown relations. When addressed in future studies, they will provide greater understanding of the origins of stereotypical attitudes and interaction in intergroup relations. The major questions that remain to be addressed are as follows.

Do foreign-born Hispanics bring negative perceptions about African Americans from their countries of origin? Do the children of foreign-born Hispanics play a role in shaping the intergroup attitudes of their parents as they encounter African Americans in school? What role do Spanish-language radio, newspapers, and television play in relations between Hispanics and African Americans? Do African Americans view Hispanics as competitors in more than just the economic sphere? Why do African American and Hispanic older women tend to have the least acceptance of closer relations between their two groups? What role can Black Hispanics play in promoting relations between African Americans and Hispanics?

Finally, the role of social class must be more adequately addressed. Although we found no statistically significant social class differences in our Houston study, standard measures of social class may not work as well with the foreign born as with the U.S. born. For instance, a fairly well-educated Mexican immigrant may be unable to use a degree from a Mexican university in many occupations in the United States. Many immigrants find their degrees unrecognized or devalued in the U.S. and must begin their education or careers at the bottom of the ladder. In addition, those who are undocumented experience an even greater inability to use education or skills on a level comparable to those who are citizens or legal residents. Thus foreign-born immigrants who are educated and skilled may have to compete for low-paying jobs with those who lack education and skills. This situation has an impact on feelings of and actual competition between groups. Importantly, however, this situation also makes it more difficult to assess social class among immigrants than among the U.S. born. The impact of social class in intergroup relations remains inadequately examined.

The implications of the findings presented in this volume for future intergroup relations across the United States depend largely on the extent to which we acknowledge the role of race in various domains of social life today. We call on today's leaders—White, African American, Hispanic, and Asian—to address the policies and institutionalized racism that lead to disparities in quality of life and competition between ethnic-racial groups. We conclude with a hopeful prediction from an African American woman:

> I can see us working together in the future. However, it won't be easy. We need people who can work together outside of negative stereotypes and perceptions. Each group has different needs, just like they are from different cultures, and this will be the biggest obstacle to get over. The only way we will be able to work together is by learning about each other's cultures and then we can get to work on the issues. The Hispanic population will be large in numbers, but they will still be dealing with being a minority in a White-dominated society. If Blacks and Hispanics could work together their power to make changes would be immense.

REFERENCES

Aboud, F. 1988. *Children and prejudice*. Cambridge, MA: Basil Blackwell.

Anzaldúa, G. 1987. *Borderlands/la frontera*. San Francisco: Spinster/Aunt Lute.

———. 1990. La consciencia de la mestiza: Towards a new consciousness. In G. Anzaldúa (ed.), *Making face, making soul/Haciendo caras: Creative and critical perspectives by feminists of color* (pp. 377–389). San Francisco: Aunt Lute Foundation Books.

Bach, R. 1993. *Changing relations: Newcomers and established residents in U.S. communities*. New York: Ford Foundation.

Bettencourt, B. A., & Bartholow, B. D. 1998. The importance of status legitimacy for intergroup attitudes among numerical minorities. *Journal of Social Issues* 54(4): 759–775.

Biernat, M., Vescio, T. K., Therno, S. A., & Crandall, C. S. 1996. Values and prejudice: Toward understanding the impact of American values on outgroup attitudes. In C. Seligman, J. M. Olson, & M. P. Zanna (eds.), *The psychology of values: The Ontario Symposium* 8 (pp. 153–189). Mahwah, NJ: Erlbaum.

Black/Hispanic dialogue. 1990. John F. Kennedy School of Government, Harvard University, October 30–31. Unpublished report of proceedings.

Blaine, B. E. 2000. *The psychology of diversity*. Mountain View, CA: Mayfield.

Bobo, L. D. 1999. Prejudice as group position: Microfoundations of a sociological approach to racism and race relations. *Journal of Social Issues* 55(3): 445–472.

Briggs, V. M., Jr. 1992. *Mass immigration and the national interest*. Armonk, NY: M. E. Sharpe.

Camaroto, S. A. 1997. *Immigration's effects on jobs and wages*. Washington, DC: Center for Immigration Studies.

———. 1998. *The wages of immigration*. Washington, DC: Center for Immigration Studies.

Cameron, J. A., Alvarez, J. M., Ruble, D. N., & Fuligni, A. J. 2001. Children's lay theories about ingroups and outgroups: Reconceptualizing research on prejudice. *Personality and Social Psychology Review* 5(2): 118–128.

Carleton, D. E. 1985. *Red scare! Right-wing hysteria, fifties fanaticism, and their legacy in Texas*. Austin: Texas Monthly Press.

Carrasco, R. 1998. Can't we all just get along? Yes. *Los Angeles Times,* June 20.

Casas, J. M., Wagenheim, B. R., Banchero, R., & Mendoza-Romero, J. 1995. Hispanic masculinity: Myth or psychological schema meriting clinical consideration. In A. M. Padilla (ed.), *Hispanic psychology* (pp. 231–244). Thousand Oaks, CA: Sage.

Castillo, A. 1994. *Massacre of the dreamers: Essays on Xicanisma*. New York: Plume.

CBS News. 1997. *New York Times* Poll, January 19.

Comas-Díaz, L. 1994. An integrative approach. In L. Comas-Díaz & B. Greene (eds.), *Women of color: Integrating ethnic and gender identities in psychotherapy* (pp. 287–318). New York: Guilford Press.

Comas-Díaz, L., & Greene, B. 1994. Overview: Connections and disconnections. In L. Comas-Díaz & B. Greene (eds.), *Women of color: Integrating ethnic and gender identities in psychotherapy* (pp. 341–346). New York: Guilford Press.

Cordova, T. 1997. Grassroots mobilization by Chicanas in the environmental and economic justice movement. *Voces: A Journal of Chicana/Latina Studies* 1(1): 32–56.

Cornelius, W. 1975. *Mexican immigration to the United States: The view from rural sending communities*. Cambridge: Department of Political Science, MIT.

Cortés, C. E. 1997. Chicanas in film: History of an image. In C. E. Rodriguez (ed.), *Latin looks: Images of Latinos and Latinas in the U.S. media* (pp. 121–141). Boulder, CO: Westview Press.

Cotera, M. 1997. Feminism: The Chicano and Anglo versions—A historical analysis. In A. M García (ed.), *Chicana Feminist Thought* (pp. 223–231). New York: Routledge.

Craig, R. B. 1971. *The bracero program*. Austin: University of Texas Press.

Crocker, J., & Luhtanen, R. 1990. Collective self-esteem and ingroup bias. *Journal of Personality and Social Psychology* 58(1): 60–67.

Cruz, J. E. 1998. *Identity and power: Puerto Rican politics and the challenge of ethnicity*. Philadelphia: Temple University Press.

Dahrendorf, R. 1959. *Class and class conflict in industrial society*. Stanford, CA: Stanford University Press.

Davila, R., & Rodriguez, N. 2000. Success and challenges of relations between African Americans and Latinos. In Comparative Human Relations Initiative, *Beyond racism* (pp. 36–48). Atlanta: Southern Education Foundation.

Davis, A. 1983. *Women, race, and class*. New York: Random House.

Davis, R. 1995. Racial difference, sin, mortality: Current trends and perspectives. In G. E. Thomas (ed.), *Race and ethnicity in America* (pp. 257–272). Washington, DC: Taylor & Francis.

Davis, S. K., & Chavez, V. 1995. Hispanic househusbands. In A. M. Padilla (ed.), *Hispanic psychology* (pp. 257–272). Thousand Oaks, CA: Sage.

DeFreitas, G. 1988. Hispanic immigration and labor market segmentation. *Industrial Relations* (Spring): 95–214.

De Leon, A. 1989. *Ethnicity in the Sunbelt: A history of Mexican Americans in Houston*. Houston: Center for Mexican American Studies, University of Houston.

———. 1993. *Mexican Americans in Texas*. Arlington Heights, IL: Harlan Davidson.

Delgado, R. 1999. *When equality ends: Stories about race and resistance*. Boulder, CO: Westview Press.

Devine, P. G. 1989. Stereotyping and prejudice: Their automatic and controlled components. *Journal of Personality and Social Psychology* 56: 5–18.

Díaz-Guerrero, R. 1987. Historical sociocultural premises and ethnic socialization. In S. J. Phinney & M. J. Rotheram (eds.), *Children's ethnic socialization, pluralism and development* (pp. 239–250). Newbury Park, CA: Sage.

Díaz-Guerrero, R., & Szalay, L. B. 1993. *El mundo subjectivo de mexicanos y norteamericanos* [The subjective world of Mexicans and North Americans]. Mexico City: Trillas.

Díaz-Loving, R., & Draguns, J. G. 1999. Culture, meaning and personality in Mexico and in the United States. In Y. T. Lee, C. R. McCauley, & J. G. Draguns (eds.), *Personality and person perception across cultures* (pp. 103–126). Mahwah, NJ: Erlbaum.

Dill, B. T. 1983. Race, class, and gender: Prospects for an all-inclusive sisterhood. *Feminist Studies* 9: 131–150.

Dovidio, J. F., Gaertner, S. L., & Validzic, A. 1998. Intergroup bias: Status, differentiation, and common in-group identity. *Journal of Personality and Social Psychology* 75(1): 109–120.

Duck, J. M., Hogg, M. A., & Terry, D. J. 2000. The perceived impact of persuasive messages on "us" and "them." In D. J. Terry & M. A. Hogg (eds.), *Attitudes, behavior, and the social context: The role of norms and group membership* (pp. 265–293). Mahwah, NJ: Erlbaum.

Dyer, J., Vedlitz, A., & Worchel, S. 1989. Social distance among racial and ethnic groups in Texas: Some demographic correlates. *Social Science Quarterly* 70(3): 607–616.

Eberstein, I. W. 1995. Social background, risk, and racial/ethnic differentials in infant mortality. In G. E. Thomas (ed.), *Race and ethnicity in America* (pp. 173–186). Washington, DC: Taylor & Francis.

Espín, O. M. 1994. Feminist approaches. In L. Comas-Díaz & B. Greene (eds.), *Women of color: Integrating ethnic and gender identities in psychotherapy* (pp. 265–286). New York: Guilford Press.

Essed, P. 1990. *Everyday racism: Reports from women of two cultures*. Alameda, CA: Hunter House.

Esses, V. M., Haddock, G., & Zanna, M. P. 1993. Mood and the expression of ethnic stereotypes. *Journal of Personality and Social Psychology* 69: 1052–1068.

Esses, V. M., Jackson, J. M., & Armstrong, T. L. 1998. Intergroup competition and attitudes toward immigrants and immigration: An instrumental model of group conflict. *Journal of Social Issues* 54(4): 699–724.

Facio, E. 1996. *Older Chicanas.* Newbury Park, CA: Sage.

Feagin, J. R. 1988. *Free enterprise city: Houston in political-economic perspective.* New Brunswick, NJ: Rutgers University Press.

———. 2000. *Racist America: Roots, current realities, and future reparations.* New York: Routledge.

Feagin, J. R., Vera, H., & Batur, P. 2001. *White racism.* 2d ed. New York: Routledge.

Ferris, S. 1994. Bus driver berated Spanish speakers, suit says. *Detroit Free Press,* June 29.

Fiske, S. T., & Taylor, S. E. 1991. *Social cognition.* New York: McGraw-Hill.

Flores-Ortiz, Y. G. 1993. La mujer y la violencia: A culturally based model for understanding and treatment. In *Mujeres Activas en Letras y Cambio Social (MALCS), Chicana critical issues* (pp. 169–182). Berkeley, CA: Third Woman Press.

———. 1995. Psychotherapy with Chicanas at midlife: Cultural/clinical considerations. In J. Adleman & G. Enguídanos (eds.), *Racism in the lives of women* (pp. 251–260). New York: Harrington Park Press.

———. 1997. The broken covenant: Incest in the Latino family. *Voces: A Journal of Chicana/Latina Studies* 1(2): 48–70.

Fox, M., & Parsel, J. S. 1994. *Immigration and immigrants.* Washington, DC: Urban Institute.

Gaertner, S. L., Mann, J. A., Dovidio, J. F., Murrell, A. J., & Pomare, M. 2000. How does cooperation reduce intergroup bias? In C. Stangor (ed.), *Stereotypes and prejudice* (pp. 435–450). Philadelphia: Psychology Press.

Gaertner, S. L., Rust, M. C., Dovidio, J. F., Bachman, B. A., & Anastasio, P. A. 1994. The contact hypothesis: The role of common ingroup identity on reducing intergroup bias. *Small Groups Research* 25: 224–249.

Gallup, CNN. 1995. *U.S.A. Today* Poll, January.

Garcia, A. M. 1989. The development of Chicana feminist discourse, 1970–1980. *Gender & Society* 3(2): 217–238.

Gilkes, C. T. 1994. "If it wasn't for the women . . .": African American women, community work, and social change. In M. Baca Zinn & B. Thornton Dill (eds.), *Women of color in U.S. society* (pp. 229–246). Philadelphia: Temple University Press.

Gordon, A. F., & Newfield, C. (eds.). 1997. *Mapping multiculturalism.* Minneapolis: University of Minnesota Press.

Green, C. 1997. *Globalization and survival in the Black diaspora: The new urban challenge.* Albany: State University of New York Press.

Guevara, L. V. 1996. *Dallas in transition: The politics of Hispanics and African Americans in the 1990s.* Claremont, CA: Tomás Rivera Policy Institute.

Gurin, P., Hurtado, A., & Peng, T. 1994. Group contacts and ethnicity in the social identities of Mexicanos and Chicanos. *Personality and Social Psychology Bulletin* 20(5): 521–532.

Gurwitt, R. 1993. Collision in Brown and Black. *Governing* 6(4): 32–36.

Hagan, J., Rodriguez, R., & Capps, R. 1999. *Effects of the 1996 Immigration and Welfare Reform Acts on communities in Texas and Mexico.* Working Paper Series 99-5. Houston: Center for Immigration Research, University of Houston.

Helmreich, W. B. 1997. *The things they say behind our back: Stereotypes and the myths behind them.* New Brunswick, NJ: Transaction.

Hewstone, M. 2000. Contact and categorization: Social psychological interventions to change intergroup relations. In C. Stangor (ed.), *Stereotypes and prejudice* (pp. 394–418). Philadelphia: Psychology Press.

hooks, b. 1984. *Feminist theory: From margin to center.* Boston: South End Press.

Hossfeld, K. J. 1994. Hiring immigrant women: Silicon Valley's "simple formula." In M. B. Zinn & B. T. Dill (eds.), *Women of color in U.S. society* (pp. 65–94). Philadelphia: Temple University Press.

Houston Chronicle. 2001. Census study: White flight soars. April 15.

Houston Independent School District. 1988. *District and Schools Profiles, 1987–88.* Houston, TX.

———. 2000. *District and Schools Profiles, 1999–2000.* Houston, TX: HSID.

Hughes, D. 1997. Racist thinking and thinking about race: What children know but don't say. *Ethos* 25(1): 117–125.

Humphrey, N. D. 1945. The stereotypes and the social types of Mexican-American youths. *Journal of Social Psychology* 22: 69–78.

Johnson, J. H., Jr., Farrell, W. C., Jr., & Guinn, C. 1997. Immigration reform and the browning of America: Tensions, conflicts, and community instability in metropolitan Los Angeles. *International Migration Review* 31(4): 1055–1095.

Johnson, J. H., Jr., & Oliver, M. L. 1994. Interethnic minority conflict in urban America: The effect of economic and social dislocations. In F. L. Pincus & H. J. Ehrlich (eds.), *Race and ethnic conflict* (pp. 194–205). Boulder, CO: Westview Press.

Jones, J. M. 1997. *Prejudice and racism.* 2d ed. New York: McGraw-Hill.

Jussim, L. J., McCauley, C. R., & Lee, Y. T. 1995. Why study stereotype accuracy and inaccuracy? In Y. T. Lee, L. J. Jussim, & C. R. McCauley (eds.), *Stereotype accuracy: Toward appreciating group differences* (pp. 3–28). Washington, DC: American Psychological Association.

Kaiser Family Foundation, National Association of Black Journalists. 1998. Blacks, Media and Health Survey, July 31.

Katz, D., & Braly, K. 1933. Racial stereotypes of one hundred college students. *Journal of Abnormal and Social Psychology* 28: 280–290.

Klineberg, S. L. 1996. *Houston's ethnic communities.* Houston, TX: Department of Sociology, Rice University.

————. 1999. The Houston Area Survey. Houston, TX: Department of Sociology, Rice University.

Kochman, T. 1987. The ethnic component in Black language and culture. In S. J. Phinney & M. J. Rotheram (eds.), *Children's ethnic socialization, pluralism and development* (pp. 219–238). Newbury Park, CA: Sage.

Lee, Y. T., Jussim, L. J., & McCauley, C. R. 1995. *Stereotype accuracy: Toward appreciating group differences.* Washington, DC: American Psychological Association.

Leyens, J. P., Yzerbyt, V., & Schadron, G. 1994. *Stereotypes and social cognition.* London: Sage.

Lippmann, W. 1922. *Public opinion.* New York: Harcourt, Brace and World.

Loewen, J. W. 1995. *Lies my teacher told me: Everything your American history textbook got wrong.* New York: New Press.

Luhtanen, R., & Crocker, J. 1992. A collective self-esteem scale: Self-evaluation of one's social identity. *Personality and Social Psychology Bulletin* 18: 302–318.

Manstead, A. S. R. 2000. The role of moral norm in the attitude-behavior relations. In D. T. Terry & M. A. Hogg (eds.), *Attitudes, behavior, and social context: The role of norms and group membership* (pp. 11–30). Mahwah, NJ: Erlbaum.

McArthur, L. Z., & Baron, R. M. 1983. Toward an ecological theory of social perception. *Psychological Review* 90: 215–238.

Mindiola, T., Jr. 1982. The perceptions of workers and supervisors at the Maxwell House coffee plant, Houston, Texas. Unpublished research report.

————. 1992. Congressional District 29. Unpublished exit poll results, Center for Mexican American Studies, University of Houston, March.

Mindiola, T., Jr., Rodriguez, N., & Niemann, Y. F. 1996. *Intergroup relations between Hispanics & African Americans in Harris County.* Houston, TX: Center for Mexican American Studies, University of Houston.

Mindiola, T., Jr., & Santos, A. 1999. City Council District H. Unpublished exit poll results, Center for Mexican American Studies, University of Houston, November.

Miranda, A. 1997. *Hombres y machos.* Boulder, CO: Westview Press.

Mirandé, A., & Enríquez, E. 1979. *La Chicana: The Mexican-American woman.* Chicago: University of Chicago Press.

Mitchell, J. L. 1993. Many Blacks in L.A. study for bilingual future. *Los Angeles Times,* December 20.

NBC News. 1999. *Wall Street Journal* Poll, March.

Niemann, Y. F. 1999. Social ecological contexts and prejudice between Hispanics and Blacks. In P. Wong (ed.), *Race, ethnicity, and nationality in the United States: Toward the twenty-first century.* Boulder, CO: Westview Press.

————. 2001. Stereotypes about Chicanas and Chicanos: Implications for counseling. *Counseling Psychologist* 29(1): 55–90.

————. n.d. A pedagogical model for engendering acceptance of cultural group differences: Combining the principles of Asch and Freire for effective teaching. Unpublished manuscript.

Niemann, Y. F., & Dovidio, J. 1998. Relationship of solo status, academic rank, and perceived distinctiveness to job satisfaction of racial/ethnic minorities. *Journal of Applied Psychology* 83(1): 55–71.

Niemann, Y. F., & Jennings, L. 1995. The role of social ecological forces and stereotypes in understanding meaning shift across ethnic and gender groups. Paper presented at the annual meeting of the American Psychological Association, New York, August.

Niemann, Y. F., Jennings, L., Rozelle, R. M., Baxter, J. C., & Sullivan, E. 1994. Use of free response and cluster analysis to determine stereotypes of eight groups. *Personality and Social Psychology Bulletin* 20(4): 379–390.

Niemann, Y. F., O'Connor, E., & McLorie, R. 1998. Intergroup stereotypes of working class Blacks and Whites: Implications for stereotype threat. *Western Journal of Black Studies* 22(2): 103–108.

Niemann, Y. F., Pollak, K., Rogers, S., & O'Connor, E. 1998. The effects of physical context on stereotyping of Hispanic males. *Hispanic Journal of Behavioral Sciences* 20(3): 349–362.

Niemann, Y. F., Romero, A., Arrendondo, J., & Rodriguez, V. 1999. What does it mean to be Mexican? Social construction of an ethnic identity. *Hispanic Journal of Behavioral Sciences* 21(1): 47–60.

Niemann, Y. F., & Secord, P. 1995. The social ecology of stereotyping. *Journal for the Theory of Social Behavior* 25(1): 1–14.

Nyamathi, A., & Vasquez, R. 1995. Impact of poverty, homelessness, and drugs on Hispanic women at risk for HIV infection. In A. M. Padilla (ed.), *Hispanic psychology: Critical issues in theory and research* (pp. 213–230). Thousand Oaks, CA: Sage.

Oakes, P. J., Haslam, S. A., & Turner, J. C. 1994. *Stereotyping and social reality.* Oxford: Blackwell.

Ochoa, G. 1999. Everyday ways of resistance and cooperation. *Frontiers: A Journal of Women's Studies* 20(1): 1–20.

Pardo, M. 1990. Mexican American women, grassroots community activists: Mothers of East Los Angeles. *Frontiers: A Journal of Women's Studies* 11(1): 1–7.

Peffley, M., & Hurwitz, J. 1998. Whites' stereotypes of blacks: Sources and political consequences. In J. Hurwitz & M. Peffley (eds.), *Perception and prejudice: Race and politics in the United States* (pp. 58–99). New Haven, CT: Yale University Press.

Pesquera, B. M., & Segura, D. M. 1993. There is no going back: Chicanas and feminism. In *Mujeres Activas en Letras y Cambio Social (MALCS), Chicana critical issues* (pp. 95–116). Berkeley, CA: Third Woman Press.

Phillips, J. A., & Massey, D. S. 1999. The new labor market: Immigration and wages after IRCA. *Demography* 36(2): 233–246.

Phinney, J. S. 1990. Ethnic identity in adolescents and adults: Review of research. *Psychological Bulletin* 108: 499–514.

———. 1991. Ethnic identity and self-esteem: A review and integration. *Hispanic Journal of Behavioral Sciences* 13: 193–208.

Purser, P. 1992. *Minority settlement patterns in the Houston area*. Center for Public Policy Publication, 92-03. Houston, TX: University of Houston.

Reisler, M. 1976. *By the sweat of their brow*. Westport, CT: Greenwood Press.

Richards, E. S. 1950. Attitudes of college students in the Southwest toward ethnic groups in the United States. *Sociology and Social Research* 35: 22–30.

Rodriguez, M. R. 1997. (En)Countering domestic violence, complicity, and definitions of Chicana womanhood. *Voces: A Journal of Chicana/Latina Studies* 1(2): 104–141.

Rodriguez, N. P. 1995. The real "new world order": The globalization of racial and ethnic relations in the late twentieth century. In M. P. Smith & J. R. Feagin (eds.), *The bubbling cauldron: Race, ethnicity and the urban crisis* (pp. 211–225). Minneapolis: University of Minnesota Press.

———. 1996. U.S. immigration and intergroup relations in the late 20th century: African Americans and Latinos. *Social Justice* 23(3): 111–124.

———. 1999. U.S. immigration and intergroup relations in the late 20th century: African Americans and Latinos. In S. Jonas & S. D. Thomas (eds.), *Immigration: A civil rights issue for the Americas* (pp. 131–144). Wilmington, DE: Scholarly Resources.

Rodriguez, N. P., Elizondo, N., Mena, D., Rojas, R., Vasquez, A., & Yeverino, F. 1994. Political mobilization in Houston's Magnolia. In R. O. de la Garza, M. Menchaca, & L. De Sipio (eds.), *Barrio ballots: Latino politics in the 1990 elections* (pp. 83–114). Boulder, CO: Westview Press.

Rodriguez, N., Ramirez, M., & Korman, M. 1999. The transmission of family values across generations of Mexican, Mexican American and Anglo American families: Implications for mental health. In R. H. Sheets & E. R. Hollins (eds.), *Racial and ethnic identity in school practices: Aspects of human development* (pp. 141–155). Mahwah, NJ: Erlbaum.

Rogers, G. O. 1995. Environmental racism or inequity: Comparative study of four ethnic groups. In G. E. Thomas (ed.), *Race and ethnicity in America* (pp. 187–204). Washington, DC: Taylor & Francis.

Rolison, G. L., & Keith, V. M. 1995. Drugs, crime, murder, and the underclass: An analysis of aggregate data from the largest metropolitan areas. In G. E. Thomas (ed.), *Race and ethnicity in America* (pp. 129–144). Washington, DC: Taylor & Francis.

Romero, G., & Wyatt, G. 1999. The prevalence and circumstances of child sexual abuse among Latina women. *Hispanic Journal of Behavioral Sciences* 21(3): 351–365.

Romo, R. 1983. *East Lost Angeles: History of a barrio*. Austin: University of Texas Press.

Romo, R., & Rodriguez, N. 1993. *Houston evaluation of community priorities: Summary report*. Claremont, CA: Tomás Rivera Center.

Root, M. P. P. 1992. The impact of trauma on personality: The second reconstruction. In L. S. Brown & M. Ballou (eds.), *Personality and psychopathology: Feminist reappraisals* (pp. 229–265). New York: Guilford Press.

Rothbart, M., & Johon, O. P. 2000. Social categorization and behavioral episodes: A cognitive analysis of the effects of intergroup contact. In C. Stangor (ed.), *Stereotypes and prejudice* (pp. 419–434). Philadelphia: Psychology Press.

Rotheram, M. J., & Phinney, J. S. 1987. Definition and perspectives in the study of children's ethnic socialization. In S. J. Phinney & M. J. Rotheram (eds.), *Children's ethnic socialization, pluralism and development*. Newbury Park, CA: Sage.

San Miguel, G., Jr. 2001. *Brown, not white*. College Station: Texas A&M University Press.

Sándor, G. 1994. The "other" Americans. *American Demographics* (June): 36–43.

Santos, A. 1999. Affirmative action in the city of Houston: The role of Hispanics. Unpublished paper presented at the Hispanics in Houston conference, Center for Mexican American Studies, University of Houston.

Schaefer, R. T. 1990. *Racial and ethnic groups*. Glenview, IL: Scott, Foresman/Little, Brown Higher Education.

Schwartz, S. H., & Struch, N. 1989. Values, stereotypes, and intergroup antagonism. In D. Bar-Tal, C. F. Graumann, A. W. Kruglanski, & W. Stroebe (eds.), *Stereotyping and prejudice: Changing conceptions* (pp. 151–168). New York: Springer-Verlag.

Sears, D. O. 1986. College sophomores in the laboratory: Influences of a narrow data base on social psychology's view of human nature. *Journal of Personality and Social Psychology* 51(3): 515–530.

Segura, D. A. 1994. Inside the work worlds of Chicana and Mexican immigrant women. In M. B. Zinn & B. T. Dill (eds.), *Women of color in U.S. society* (pp. 95–112). Philadelphia: Temple University Press.

Shankman, A. 1978. Black on Yellow: Afro-Americans view Chinese-Americans, 1850–1935. *Phylon* 39(1): 1–17.

Shelton, B. A., Rodriguez, N. P., Feagin, J. R., Bullard, R. D., & Thomas, R. D. 1989. *Houston: Growth and decline in a Sunbelt boomtown*. Philadelphia: Temple University Press.

Sherif, M. 1966. *In common predicament: Social psychology of intergroup conflict and cooperation*. Boston: Houghton Mifflin.

Simon, B., & Brown, R. 2000. Perceived intragroup homogeneity in minority-majority contexts. In C. Stangor (ed.), *Stereotypes and prejudice* (pp. 326–337). Philadelphia: Psychology Press.

Stangor, C., & Shaller, M. 2000. Stereotypes as individual and collective representations. In C. Stangor (ed.), *Stereotypes and prejudice* (pp. 64–82). Philadelphia: Psychology Press.

Stavans, I. 1996. The Latin phallus. In R. Gonzalez (ed.), *Muy macho: Latino men confront their manhood* (pp. 143–164). New York: Anchor Books.

Stephan, W. G., & Finlay, K. 1999. The role of empathy in improving intergroup relations. *Journal of Social Issues* 55(4): 729–744.

Tajfel, H. 1969. Cognitive aspects of prejudice. *Journal of Social Issues* 25: 79–97.

Tajfel, H., & Turner, J. C. 1986. The social identity theory of intergroup behavior. In S. Worchel & W. G. Austin (eds.), *Psychology of intergroup relations,* 2d ed. (pp. 7–24). Chicago: Nelson-Hall.

Terry, D. J., Hogg, M. A., & White, K. M. 2000. Attitude-behavior relations: Social identity and group membership. In D. T. Terry & M. A. Hogg (eds.), *Attitudes, behavior, and social context: The role of norms and group membership* (pp. 67–94). Mahwah, NJ: Erlbaum.

Texas Bureau of Vital Statistics. 1998. Texas Department of Health. Austin.

Thomas, M. E., Herring, C., & Horton, H. D. 1995. Racial and gender differences in returns from education. In G. E. Thomas (ed.), *Race and ethnicity in America* (pp. 239–254). Washington, DC: Taylor & Francis.

Tienda, M., & Singer, A. 1995. Wage mobility of undocumented workers in the United States. *International Migration Review* (Spring): 1–21.

Time, CNN. 1995. *U.S.A. Today* Poll, January.

———. 1996. Yankelovich Partners Poll, July.

———. 1998. Yankelovich Partners Poll, October 16.

Tobar, H. 1992. Blacks, Latinos coexist in a peace tempered by fear. *Los Angeles Times,* February 19.

Torres, A. 1995. *Between melting pot and mosaic: African Americans and Puerto Ricans in the New York political economy.* Philadelphia: Temple University Press.

Trager, H. G., & Yarrow, M. R. 1952. *They learn what they live: Prejudice in young children.* New York: Harper & Brothers.

U.S. Census Bureau. 1972. *Census of population and housing: 1970, census tracts.* Final Report PHC (1)-89. Houston Texas SMSA, Washington, DC: Government Printing Office.

———. 1983. *1980 census of population and housing, census tracts, Houston, Tex.* PHC80-2-184. Washington, DC: Government Printing Office.

———. 1993. *1990 census of population and housing, population and Houston characteristics for census tracts and block numbering areas, Houston-Galveston-Brazoria, TX, CMSA (Part), Houston, TX PMSA.* 1990 CPH-3-176C. Washington, DC: Government Printing Office.

———. 1995. *Mothers who receive food stamps.* Statistic Brief 95-122. Washington, DC.

———. 1998. *Statistical abstract of the United States: 1998.* 118th ed. Washington, DC: Government Printing Office.

———. 2000a. *2000 American Community Survey Profile for Houston City, Texas.* http://www.census.gov/acs/www/Products/Profiles/2000/index.htm

———. 2000b. *Statistical abstract of the United States: 2000.* Washington, DC: Government Printing Office.

———. 2001a. Census 2000 PHC-T-C. Population by race and Hispanic or Latino origin for the United States, regions, divisions, states, Puerto Rico, and places of 100,000 or more population. Internet release date: April 2, 2001. http://blue.census.gov/population/www/cen2000/phc-t6.html

———. 2001b. The Hispanic population: Census 2000 brief. Issued May 2001. C2KBR/01-3. www.census.gov/population/www/socdemo/hispanic.html

Valdez, A. 1999. The implications of intermarriage trends among Mexican Americans in Houston. Unpublished paper presented at the Hispanics in Houston conference, Center for Mexican American Studies, University of Houston.

Van Ausdale, D., & Feagin, J. R. 2001. *The first R: How children learn race and racism.* Lanham, MD: Rowman & Littlefield.

Vasquez, M. J. T. 1984. Power and status of the Chicana: A social-psychological perspective. In J. L. Martinez & R. H. Mendoza (eds.), *Chicano psychology* (pp. 269–288). Orlando, FL: Academic Press.

———. 1995. Latinas. In L. Comas-Díaz & B. Greene (eds.), *Women of color: Integrating ethnic and gender identities in psychotherapy* (pp. 114–138). New York: Guilford Press.

Vaughan, G. M. 1987. A social psychological model of ethnic identity development. In S. J. Phinney & M. J. Rotheram (eds.), *Children's ethnic socialization, pluralism and development* (pp. 73–91). Newbury Park, CA: Sage.

Winborne, W., & Cohen, R. 1998. Intergroup relations in the United States: Research perspectives. New York: National Conference for Community and Justice.

Worchel, S. 1999. *Written in blood: Ethnic identity and the struggle for human harmony.* New York: Worth.

Zavella, P. 1987. *Women's work and Chicano families: Cannery workers of the Santa Clara Valley.* Ithaca, NY: Cornell University Press.

INDEX

deportation, 2

Desegregation Act, 59

discrimination, 20, 23, 65, 109, 120, 121, 122; against African Americans, 58, 100; against Hispanics, 56, 57, 77, 80; by Mexican Americans against other Hispanics, 113; common experiences of, among Hispanics and African Americans, 92, 95, 105, 126–127; defenses against, 72; overcoming, 102; protection against, for lesbians and gays, 98. *See also* prejudice, racism

dropout rates, 23, 29

education, 62, 63, 95, 122; higher, 21–22; improving access to and quality of, 105, 109, 121; lack of, among Hispanics, 19, 23; lack of, in women of color, 90; levels of, in survey respondents, 6. *See also* bilingual education; dropout rates; Houston Independent School District

employment. *See* jobs

English language, 38, 108

English Only movement, 52, 88

environmental hazards, 90

essentialist reasoning, 68

fear, 69, 73, 77; as a component of race relations, 59, 63; of African Americans by Hispanics, 66, 81, 121; of Hispanics by African Americans, 102–103, 120

family, 100–101, 109, 120; in Hispanic culture, 58

feminist approach, 73–93

food stamps, 80

Fort Bend County (Texas), 125

Fourth Ward, 13

Garifuna, 113

gay rights, 98–99, 109, 120

Georgia (state of), 1, 111

Gore, Al, 105

government programs, 126; inadequacy of, 99–100; perception of favoritism in, 47–50, 64, 77, 82, 118

Guatemala, 113

guest worker program, 63

Harris County (Texas), 5, 55, 125. *See also* Houston

Head Start program, 49

health care, 88–89, 95, 105, 121, 122

Honduras, 113

housing, 12–13, 90, 95, 105. *See also* integration (residential)

Houston, 44–47, 88, 95, 102, 117, 124–125; affirmative action in, 49, 64; city council, 15, 105; impact of Hispanic immigration on, 3, 50–51, 56, 111, 114, 115, 116, 118; intergroup relations in, 6–17, 104–105, 130, 131; politics in, 105–109, 112, 113; as a research setting, 4, 43

Houston Area Survey, 5, 98

Houston Independent School District (HISD), 12, 15, 16–17, 105, 115

"Houston Proud," 124

identity, 36, 82–83

immigration, 37, 44, 45, 104, 108, 112, 113, 117, 120; attitudes toward, 62; impact of, on Houston, 4, 9, 11–15, 50, 51–52, 63, 73, 77, 82, 115, 118; increase of, in Houston, xi, 123, 130; limits on, 2; policies, 27; undocumented, 101–102

incest, 91

income, 6, 9, 62, 63, 95, 125–126

Independents (political), 107, 108

index of dissimilarity, 44

infant mortality, 90

integration (residential), 62

among Hispanics, against African Americans, 103, 120; common experiences of, among African Americans and Hispanics, 92, 126–127; derivation of, 87; perceptions about, 73, 77, 81, 109; reducing, 128, 130. See also discrimination; racism
Proposition 187 (California), 118
Protestantism, 98
public schools, 114. See also education; Houston Independent School District
public sector, 3, 100

racial profiling, 23
racism, 85–89, 116, 119; awareness of, in African Americans, 72, common experiences of, among African Americans and Hispanics, 83, 92; as discussed in history texts, 24–25; in language, 22; and the media, 29; and stereotypes, 20–22. See also discrimination; prejudice
radio. See media
Rainbow Coalition, xii
recession (economic), 12–13
redistricting, 129
redlining, 23
religion, 96, 98. See also Catholicism
Republican party, 107, 108
residential areas. See housing
Rice University, 5

Salvadorans, 5
Sanchez, Orlando, 17, 105–106, 131
Santa Anna, Antonio López de, 7
Scholastic Aptitude Test (SAT), 50
segregation, 21; efforts to end, 9, 10, 104; promotion of, through Jim Crowism, 8; residential, 44; in schools, 25, 126
self-esteem, 36, 39, 84. See also Collective Self-Esteem Scale

sexism, 83, 89–91
sexual abuse, 91
sexuality (in Hispanic culture), 98–99
sexual-racial objectification, 90
slavery, 7, 21, 25, 40, 86, 126
social class, 62–63, 71, 85, 125–126, 131–132
social ecologies, 22–24
social mobility, 117
social science research, 26–27, 67
socialization, 70, 87
Spanish language, 12, 13, 50; as a cause of friction between Hispanics and African Americans, xii, 14–15, 52, 64, 88, 118; monolingual speakers of, 47, 168; stereotypes associated with, 31; in the workplace, 63, 104
state legislature (Texas), 15, 105
status legitimacy, 86–87
stereotypes, xiii, 4, 38, 42n.1, 87; anti-Black, 81, 103; flexibility of, 122; implications of, for intergroup relations, 19–41, 116, 121; as portrayed in the media, 71; reduction of negative, 117
suburbs, 44
suffrage (women's), 91–92

teenage mothers, 100
television. See media
Third Ward, 13, 116
third world countries, 92
Tomas Rivera Center, 5

unemployment benefits, 100
University of California, 50
University of Texas School of Public Health, 88
U.S. Census Bureau, 2, 3
U.S. Congress, 59, 106–107, 115
U.S. Constitution, 52, 96
U.S. Immigration Act (1996), 118